KALAPAHAD

KALAPAHAD
Aswini Kumar Ghose

Translated by
Bhagabat Nath

BLACK EAGLE BOOKS
Dublin, USA | Bhubaneswar, India

Black Eagle Books
USA address:
7464 Wisdom Lane
Dublin, OH 43016

India address:
E/312, Trident Galaxy, Kalinga Nagar,
Bhubaneswar-751003, Odisha, India

E-mail: info@blackeaglebooks.org
Website: www.blackeaglebooks.org

First International Edition Published by
Black Eagle Books, 2025

KALAPAHAD
by **Aswini Kumar Ghose**
Translated by **Bhagabat Nath**

Original Copyright © **Aswini Kumar Ghose**
Translation Copyright © **Bhagabat Nath**

All rights reserved. No part of this publication may be reproduced, stored in a retrieval system, or transmitted, in any form or by any means, electronic, mechanical, photocopying, recording or otherwise without the prior permission of the publisher.

Cover & Interior Design: Ezy's Publication

ISBN- 978-1-64560-800-4 (Paperback)

Printed in the United States of America

Introduction

The authority of colonial powers is always challenged by the colonized peoples for their imposition of imperialistic culture and language, exploitation and discrimination. Colonial rule leads to resistance. Beyond the violent/non-violent binary, colonial resistance is expressed through organised demands for equality and freedom, revolts, mass protests, and movements aimed at achieving independence. This term, colonial resistance, underscores the persistent efforts by the "Other" to assert their autonomy and identity *vis-a-vis* imperial authority.

During the colonial era in India it was very arduous to raise one's voice against the powerful British imperialists. Hence the intellectuals, more particularly the writers, undertook the task of creating a deep sense of patriotism amongst the common mass. In Odisha some powerful litterateurs like Fakir Mohan Senapati in prose; Radhanath Ray, Madhusudan Rao and Gangadhar Meher in poetry were the pioneers in this regard. Because of these writers Odia language could assert its independent status.

Vyasakabi Fakir Mohan Senapati's works are characterized by the realistic portrayal of Odia society, particularly its rural life and the struggles of common people, political landscape of colonial Odisha, the themes of social change, displacement, and the impact of the British Empire on ordinary lives.

Kabibar Radhanath Ray denounced despots, tyrants and oppressors. He depicted social problems. He had a spirit of protest against conventional morality, a disbelief in the power of gods and goddesses. He is the first major poet to turn to the scenic beauty of rural Orissa. His description of lakes, rivers, and valleys of Orissa were extremely colourful and appealing. His works attracted love of the Odias to the natural panorama of Odisha.

Bhakta Kabi Madhusudan Rao is considered the father of modern Oriya lyric. His poetry is charged with profound religious emotions. He replaced the old lyrical forms like the *chautisa, koili boli, padia,* etc. by odes, elegies, sonnets and other forms of Western poetry. He is also regarded as a great mystic poet as he sees divinity in every being. The mystic Madhusudan later turned from the religious themes to the patriotic and the nationalistic themes.

Swabhab Kabi Gangadhar Meher used his poetry to critique societal injustices, promote patriotism, and offer guidance on moral living. His poems are known for their simplicity, moral depth, and ability to connect the readers on various levels with the glorious past and the prevailing pitiable condition of the motherland. The poets of Satyabadi group also started working in a planned way in this direction.

The playwrights took up historical, mythological, social themes. Through historical plays they tried to enliven the present population with the heroic deeds of their forefathers. The British rulers did not bother at first to restrict the writer class as outwardly these literary works seemed to be very unharmful to them. But like a powerful drug these literary works started influencing the people inwardly. Thus, the writers achieved their goal of precipitating colonial resistance without offending the rulers.

Aswini Kumar Ghose who entered the dramatic arena at this crucial juncture took no time to survey the entire atmosphere and immediately followed the path, created by his predecessors. He wrote *Bhishma, Srimandira, Chandaluni* to preach the message of national integration. His works *Seojee, Kalapahad, Govinda Vidyadhara, Kapilendra Dev, Konark* carried messages for propagation of the cause of patriotism. Just like mythological and historical dramas, his social plays were also equally powerful. Some such plays entitled *Chasa Jhia* (*Farmer's Daughter*), *Sri Lokanath, Dukhe Sukhe* (*Through Ups and Downs*) and *Abhinaya* (*Acting*) are still remembered with nostalgia by the drama loving people.

Aswini Kumar Ghose (1892–1962) is an eminent Odia theatre personality. He is related to two illustrious sons of Odisha: Karmaveer Gourishankar Ray was his maternal grandfather and Ramshankar Ray, the pioneer Oriya dramatist, was his maternal granduncle. His dramas can be divided into three categories namely mythological, historical and social. His mythological and devotional plays are *Bhishma, Sabitri, Salbeg, Dasia Bauri, Tyagi Ram Das, Sri Mandira, Raghu Arakhit, Bandhu Mohanty, Chandaluni, Janaki, Sakhigopal, Satyanarayan*. His historical plays include *Seojee, Kalapahad, Govinda Vidyadhar, Samaleswari, Utkala Seojee, Kalapahad, Govinda Vidyadhar, Samaleswari, Utkala Gaurav, Konark, Kesari Ganga, Paikapua, Tajmahal, Odiajhia, Bhanja Bhunjanga, Kapilendradev, Bhubaneswar*. His social plays are *Hindu Ramani, Masterbabu, Irani, Bhai, Sri Lokanath, Chasa Jhia, Mamalatkar, Abhinay, Dukhe Sukhe*, and *Kaidi*.

A versatile genius, Aswini Kumar Ghose wrote almost 41 full-fledged plays in Odia, two plays in Bengali, four novels in Odia, apart from two farces, some one-act plays, radio plays and gramophone record plays. He produced plays of various types — tragedy, comedy, tragi-comedy, farces etc. He has a wide thematic choice that incorporated mythology, history, biography, social life. He was quite popular with his audience for blending the religious elements with the supernatural ones, humanizing the divine and elevating man to a high moral and spiritual level. His straight forward language also easily impressed the common mass. He studied intimately the psychology of the average Oriya audience and gave them what they cherished most.

The traditional account of Kalapahad, a Hindu renegade and an iconoclast has influenced the Odia social and literary space. According to some historical documents, his original name was Rajiv Lochan Ray or Kalachand Roy Bhadury, a Bengali (Barendra Brahmin) who fell in love with Dulari, the beautiful and charming daughter of Sulaiman Karrani, the Nawab of Bengal. He married her after his conversion to Islam. But he repented of his deed as he faced boycott in the society. Therefore, he wanted to return to Hinduism. But the Hindu society refused to accept him as a Hindu. At last, he came to the Temple of Lord Jagannath at Puri to perform expiation to convert himself to Hinduism. But the priests scornfully turned down his prayer for conversion. He got enraged and assumed the name of Kalapahad and vowed to ruin Hindu religion, images and temples.

Madalapanji, the temple chronicle holds that Kalapahad desecrated the Jagannath temple. According to this tradition, "when the servitors of the temple heard of Kalapahad's design on the temple, they took the images out of the temple and hid them at a place named Hatipada near Chilka lake. But Kalapahad learnt of this and brought the images from that place on elephants. He carried them to the bank of river Ganges and set fire to them. Just at that time a miracle happened. His body got cracked into pieces. Being perplexed by this, he brought out the gods from the fire and dumped them in the Ganges. Holy Ganga carried the Brahma (or *Brahma Pinda*) downstream where a Vaishnava devotee Bishar Mohanty extracted the immortal part (*Brahma*). Later he consecrated the *Brahma* at Garh Kujanga temple. The 'Brahma' was worshipped there for seven years, (1568A.D to 1575 A.D). In 1575 A.D during the rule of Ramachandra Dev, the first king of the Bhoi dynasty, 'Brahma' was brought from Garh Kujang and kept at Khordha Garh by him. Next year in 1576 A.D, the construction of new images, their entry in to the temple along with the installation of 'Brahma' in them were performed. This account of Kalapahad has been mentioned by Dr. Sarat Chandra Biswal in his article, "Sri Jagannath and Kalapahad" published in *Odisha Review*.

Kalapahad is a legend in Odisha. The following poetic stanza is popular among Odia folk.

Aila Kalapahada
Bhangila luharabada
Piila Mahanadi pani,
Suvarna thalire heda parasile Mukundadevanka Rani.

It means-Kalapahad came, pulled down the iron fence, drank the water of river Mahanadi, and the queen of Raja Mukunda Deva served beef to him on a golden plate. Pyari Mohan Acharya recorded this popular saying in 1979.

The contact of the queen of Mukunda Deva with Kalapahad was well-known in Odisha in the last part of the 19th century A.D. which is stated in the *History of Odisha* in Odia by Pyarimohan Acharya which states that Kalapahad was satisfied with the pleasure of beef served by the queen of Mukunda Deva. This well-known stanza in Odisha was slightly changed by Kripasindhu Mishra as he used Hira (diamond) for Heda (beef) in his famous article entitled "Barabati Durga" which was serialized in *Mukura* (Odia monthly) from 1913. It was also found in his book entitled *Barabati Durga* both in the first and second editions. Historian G. N. Dash remarked, "The idea that the queen of Mukunda Deva, the last Hindu monarch of Orissa, ever served beef to Kalapahad (and by implication became Kalapahad's mistress) was painful, abhorrent and not acceptable to the Oriya nationalists and nationalist historians. Therefore, they replaced the word 'heda' (beef) with 'hira' (diamond), thereby suggesting that she offered diamonds to Kalapahad as a bribe and thus escaped from his clutches".

But Godavarish Mishra, contemporary and associate of Kripasindhu Mishra, did not feel it necessary to change the original poem. His masterpiece *Alekhika* (1923) contains a poem entitled "Kalapahada".

In that poem it is stated:
Aila Kalapahada, kede tana baha,
Barabatigadu bhangila luharabada
Ghadike thate ta deleta sukhei Mahanadi pani;
Subarna thalire Hedaparasile Mukunda Devanka Rani. It means – Kalapahada came; with his well-built arms, broke the iron fence from the fort Barabati. His army dried up the water of the river Mahanadi by drinking among themselves. The queen of Mukunda Deva served him beef on a golden plate.

The historians were inclined to study the Kalapahad tradition for searching its authenticity in Odisha. But Odia literature was deeply influenced by the tradition. Stories were created on the theme of Kalapahad with an imaginative vision as we find in the story of *Pradipa Nirvana* by Dayanidhi Mishra in the 1920s. Aswini Kumar Ghose in his drama *Kalapahad* (1922) captivated the nationalist Odias. Kalapahad was interpreted as a social reformer in Odisha in the long poem of 'Kalapahadi Gatha' composed by one Sri Kalapahada and was serialized in *Utkala Sahitya* (premier Odia literary monthly). This account of Kalapahad has been mentioned in his article "Social Change In Eastern India: Traditional Narrative Of Kalapahad Reinterpreted" by the historian, Kailash Chandra Dash.

An interesting historical basis of the tradition of Kalapahad's iconoclastic imaginings was his success in throwing the wooden images of Jagannatha, Balabahdra, Subhadra and Sudarsana into the fire for their destruction. Kailash Chandra Dash observes that Kalapahad completed this work of destruction of Jagannatha images because after the death of Mukunda Deva, the king of Odisha, Kalapahad might have thought that Jagannatha was the central aspect of Gajapati kingship in Odisha and that the end of Gajapati kingship in Odisha would be completed not by the death of the king who was a mere deputy of Lord Jagannatha as Jagannatha was declared the emperor of Odisha kingdom from the phase of the Ganga king Anangabhima III in the 13th century A.D. Hence, by the destruction of the images only the entire Gajapati kingship would be subverted. An interesting study on the deputy ideology of the Ganga-Gajapati kingship has been furnished by Hermann Kulke. His account of Kalapahad does not subscribe to his wanton iconoclastic image but as a political strategist.

There is a resonance of history and myth in *Kalapahad*. The action of the play is consistent with the historical tradition but the playwright has introduced several myths to appeal the sentiments of the audience. The plot of the play revolves around Kalapahad, a Hindu brahmin youth named Kalachand, who is learned in scriptures. He visits the court of the Nawab of Bengal to reclaim his property. But he falls in love with Dulia, the daughter of the Nawab, converts himself to Islam and marries the princess. He becomes the Commander-in-Chief of the Bengal army. But he could not reconcile with his new religion and part with the Hindu ways. A repentant Kalapahad comes to Puri, the seat of Lord Jagannath, to appeal to the Council of Pundits for reconversion. His Muslim wife Dulia follows him along with her handmaid Firoja to Puri. The greedy and mercenary scholars humiliate him, assault him physically and drive him out of the temple premises. They were cruel enough to offend Dulia and Firoja as infidels. The suffering is too much for Kalapahad to put up with. He vows to desecrate Hindu gods and goddesses, and demolish Hindu temples.

In the historical tradition, saga of Kalapahad is inextricably intertwined with the rise and fall of Mukunda

Deb. The plot of the play begins when the Mughal emperor Akbar extends the offer of friendship to Mukunda Deb, the Ganapati king of Odisha and seeks his help to put down the rebellion of Suleman, the Nawab of Bengal. He asks Katalu Khan, one of his Mughal Generals, to assist Mukunda Deb. But Katalu is aggrieved to serve as an assistant. Mukunda Deb is a valiant warrior. He considers action as his principal duty and self-sacrifice as his greatest pleasure. He accepts Badshah Akbar's offer and proceeds with his army to humble Suleman.

The insurgency in Bengal has been masterminded by Rahamat, the General of Bengal army. He is aggrieved as he is superseded by Kalapahad as the General when is appointed as the new General. Rahamat joins hands with Katalu Khan and ropes in Abdul, the Nawab's nephew to settle his score with Kalapahad. They plan to assassinate Mukunda Deb to fulfil Katalu Khan's design to acquire Odisha.

As the Nawab calls for Kalapahad to lead the Bengal army against the Mughal army, he is baffled to see that Kalapahad has become a changed man. He repents of his conversion and marriage to the Muslim princess. He wishes to reconvert himself. He proceeds to Puri, the seat of Lord Jagannath. Rahamat usurps his position.

In the battle between Mukunda Deb and Suleman, Suleman is defeated and is taken as a prisoner. Mukunda Deb is disappointed to find no help from Badshah Akbar and plans to visit Delhi to apprise the betrayal of Katalu to the Badshah. In the meantime, Abdul stealthily enters Mukunda Deba's camp where Suleman was resting and stabs him to death thinking him to be Mukunda Deb. Immediately he realises his blunder and repents.

Dulia is on her way to Puri to be with her husband.

She visits Tilottama, Kalapahad's Hindu wife in search of her husband at the hut in Kalapahad's village. They meet at a time when his mother breathes her last. The meeting between Dulia and Tilottama, Kalapahad's visit to his dying mother, Tolottama disguising herself as a boy named Golap and her meeting Dulia and Firoja before the Fort Barabti when Dulia was wounded by Shikhi and Manai, Mukunda Deba's queen attending on injured Dulia and her hospitality to the women, Suleman's battle with Mukunda Deb, his arrest and assassination seem to be the playwright's own innovation to fulfil the necessity of the plot and does not seem to be authenticated by historical tradition.

On return from Puri, Kalapahad accidentally kills Abdul. Dying Abdul conveys that instigated by Rahamat to stab Mukunda Deb to death while he was sleeping in his camp in the battle field, he has killed his uncle the Nawab thinking him to be Mukunda Deb while he was sleeping in Mukunda Deb's camp. Rahamat is taken as a prisoner on orders of Kalapahad. However, he later escapes. Dulia learns about her father's death from dying Abdul and Abdul dies in the arms of Dulia. She felt miserable. Kalapahad is more determined to fulfil his oath of destroying Hindu religion despite Dulia and Golap's persuasions to refrain from his sinful desires. Golap inspires Dulia to be resolute in preventing her husband from committing sin.

On his return from Delhi, while Mukunda Deb has been waiting for Mughal help in his camp in the battle field, Kalapahad attacks Mukunda Deb at night and as he is unarmed he fails to put up a fight and is taken a prisoner. With the help of Golap he escapes the prison and returns to his camp. Next Kalapahad signs a treaty of peace with Mukunda Deb. Accordingly, all Muslim soldiers are disarmed and sent back. But Mukunda Deb's aides betray him and secretly return the weapons to the Muslim soldiers. While Katalu and Rahamat are secretly conspiring against Mukunda Deb, they are shot dead by hunters.

In the meantime, Ramachandra Bhanja, the Chief of Saranga Garh, and a subordinate ruler of Mukunda Dev sends his messengers, Shikhi and Manai, offering his help to Kalapahad to attack Odisha. Kalapahad accepts the offer and proceeds to invade Odisha. Golap, Dulia and Firoja follow him in disguise.

In a hilly forest while Mukunda Deb's queen was ready to face Kalapahad, she finds his soldiers famished and exhausted, she offers them food and Kalapahad is grateful to her and does not intend to fight. But Ramachandra Bhanja appears and reminds him of his revenge and instigates him to fight the queen. An intense fight ensues. Soldiers of Utkal recede. The Queen is defeated and her General is killed. The queen and the women folk of the city immerse themselves in the water of the royal tank to avoid humiliation at the hands of Kalapahad.

Mukunda Deb returns to Odisha and finds that the Biraja Temple at Jajpur has been destroyed by Kalapahad. He learns about the death of his queen and the General, Kony Singh. He learns about the treachery of Sikhi and Manai and imprisons them. He assembles his army and returns to Cuttack.

Kalapahad attacks the Temple of Lord Jagannath. Dulia and Golap along with the priests offer a stiff resistance. Dulia is severely injured. Kalapahad escapes with image of Lord Jagannath, throws the image into a huge fire prepared by the Muslims on the sea beach. Golap recovers the image and she is severely injured. Kalapahad discovers that Golap is his Tilottama in disguise. Dulia too appears and both Dulia and Tilottama die before the helpless

Kalapahad. Shikhi and Manai enter with Mukunda Deb's cut-off head. Kalapahad is bewildered and frightened. On his orders Shikhi and Manai are executed.

The final meeting of Kalapahad with his two wives, Tilottama and Dulia, is a compromise on history as it has been nowhere mentioned in history. This is a myth created by the playwright for dramatic necessity. The play is Tragedy as the protagonist Kalapahad is stranded alone and the stage is littered with dead bodies.

The play structured like a Shakespearean Tragedy with five acts and as many scenes. The suffering of the protagonist is of tragic dimension. A great care has been taken by the translator to make the work beautiful without compromising the originality of the text.

Dr. Bhagabat Nath
Former Senior Reader in English

DRAMATIS PERSONAE

MALE

Akbar	:	Mughal Emperor
Mansingh	:	Commander-in-Chief of Akbar
Katalu Khan	:	Mughal Masabdar
Birbal	:	Court Jester
Tansen	:	Court Musician
Mukunada Dev	:	Ruler of Odisha
Koni Samanatasinghar	:	Commander-in-Chief of Odisha
Rama Chandra Bhanja	:	A Feudal Chief of Odisha
Manai Mahapatra	:	Shikhi Mahapatra & Soldiers of Odisha
Suleman	:	Nawab of Bengal
Kalapahad	:	General and Son-in-Law of Nawab
Rahamat	:	Assistant General
Abdul	:	Nawab's Nephew
		Pundits, Guards, Messenger, Watchman, Moghul Soldiers, Pathan Soldiers, Hindu Soldiers, citizens, hunters etc.

FEMALE

Indumati	:	Queen of Mukunda Dev
Dulia	:	Nawab's niece and Second wife of Kalapahad
Tilottama	:	First wife of Kalapahad
An old woman	:	Mother of Kalapahad
Firoza	:	Attendant of Dulia
Golap	:	Tilottama in man's attire
		Shadow Tilottama, Shadow Old Woman, dancers, women of the city etc.

ACT I
SCENE I

The Mughal Court in Delhi.

(*Emperor Akbar is seated on his throne. Other courtiers like Mansingh, Birbal and Katalu etc. are seated according to their station.*)

(Song)

Emperor's on the throne at court
All his nobles sit apart;
As if Queen Moon in full moon skies
Shines among her starry fays;
As if the lotus is in full bloom
    And a host of bees hover 'n hum.
Come, let's dance 'n sing in joy
Chant loudly "Jay, Jay, Jay";
Let the flame of your delight
Catch the air and the sky
Let the ripples of your joy
    Thrill all hearts with new light.

AKBAR : Dear Khan Saheb, be not needlessly moody; give up your sulk.

BIRBAL : But, Your Highness! Keep it in mind that our Radhika (*implicitly to Katalu Khan*) is rough in body and harsh in mind.
(*All burst into laughter.*)

KATALU : Birbal, it's not a theatre, it's the Court.

BIRBAL : I thought it's a battle field. However, you had done me a great favour. Had you not been there, I would not have safely returned to be face to face with His Majesty so boldly.

AKBAR	: Birbal, when we had been to invade Odisha, when we realised that it's quite impossible to occupy it, we had to retreat. Katalu had not wilfully deserted the battlefield; he had just carried out the royal orders. Warrior Katalu! Is it heroic in this case for you to be moody?
KATALU	: Your Highness, does this humble servant of yours feel sulky for himself? I care for one whose glory is yet to be tarnished and who is adulated in all corners of the world.
AKBAR	: My loyal Khan Saheb! Couldn't you yet realise my feelings for you? You couldn't rightly assess me yet.
KATALU	: Your Highness, I have really understood you; rightly measured you too. Your Highness is like a source of pure blue water covered with hard stones. Your heart is like a pot full of milk covered with skins. You appear as fearsome as a tiger on the surface, but in reality, you are as tender as an infant in arms. You are like the bright radiant sun from outside but in reality, but within you shine as the moon, cool and refreshing like nectar. This is how I have known you and understood you.
TANSEN	: Dear Khan Saheb, these are the blemishes of His Majesty. What an artisan Allah is! He has created a thing in His furnace but what he produced is just the opposite – cool as water. How wonderful!

(*Akbar and Mansingh smile.*)

KATALU	:	Certainly, dear jester! It's very wonderful. Your Highness, it's not the mocking of a jester.
AKBAR	:	(*looking at Mansingh*) Khan Saheb really feels offended.
MANSINGH	:	He wished at first to vanquish Mukunda Dev. (*aside*) Hail, Mukunda Dev. Glory be to your Kshatriya blood! (*heaving a sigh of relief*) Thereafter, he could have signed a treaty of friendship with him according to your wish.
KATALU	:	It was not my final wish. Which noble and ambitious ruler can ignore Odisha, the land of greenery, the land of fine arts, the happy hunting ground of Goddess Lakshmi and Goddess Saraswati, and whose feet are washed by the sea full of gems? Can he so easily refrain from subjugating that arrogant and valiant king Mukunda Dev of Odisha?
		(*Everybody looks at Akbar anxiously.*)
AKBAR	:	Dear Commander, is it the duty of a ruler? Is it prowess of a warrior?
KATALU	:	You ae a wise statesman. How dare I, an unwise being, make you understand it? This much I may remind you, Your Highness, it's the duty of a ruler to expand his territory. It is neither a show of heroism nor the zeal of defeating an enemy only.
COURTIER	:	You are right, Katalu! You are right.
AKBAR	:	Is it the duty of a king, dear courtiers? Is it the heroism of a warrior, Katlu Khan? If it is so, then fie on the duty of a king which

is exhibited in enriching the royal coffers by plundering the neighbouring states or far off kingdoms like a mean robber and in adding to his selfish enjoyment. Fie more on the intrepidness of a warrior who instead of engaging himself in ameliorating the impoverished condition of the sick and the suffering, the needy and the deprived, spends his energy in weakening the strength of the equals or the lowly. Fie a hundred times on his heroism. (*addressing the courtiers*) Oh kings, lend me your ears. Oh warriors, please listen to me. I will not authenticate the duty of a ruler by enhancing the wealth bequeathed to me by my forefathers as a legacy. I will not show my heroism by smearing the royal throne entrusted in good faith to me by my loyal subjects with the blood of my enemies. I'll rather submerge the enemies with the nectar of love and friendship and drench the subjects who are like my children with the shower of peace and happiness.

ALL : Long live Emperor Akbar!

MANSINGH : (*aside*) This is why this unfortunate Hindu today considers himself fortunate. It is the sole happiness of a warrior if he can worship a true warrior. This is also the chief happiness of a subject if he can serve his ruler properly.

(*Tansen enters.*)

TANSEN : (Song)

Hail, Akbar, the Lord of Bharat!
Hail, the illustrious scion of Mughals!
Hail, the Emperor, mercy incarnate!
Before you raise your arms, your enemies fall dead,
Your empire expands, without horror n bloodshed,
Hindu or Muslim all embrace in brotherhood,
With little   prejudice to caste or creed.
Rule of law in your regime righteousness obeys,
Your administering justice never favour betrays,
Forgiver to   the culprit, generous to the poor,
You ensure peace and your subjects prosper.
In this peace-loving land, you shine like the Lord,
All your glorious saga has   far and wide spread.
I sing your praise, O my lord and master,
Glory be to you, ever be of good cheer.

AKBAR : Welcome, dear Tansen. You are our cuckoo of spring.

TANSEN : Is this humble servant only a cuckoo in spring?

AKBAR : Certainly not. I don't mean that you follow spring; spring follows you. Spring is eternally present with me as long as you are beside me. How pious and heavenly is your melodious song! It is like a fountain to drench the parched ears. Hearing it, heart leaps up in joy and new inspiration springs up. I feel that I am without strength and you are my giver of energy; I am ignorant and you are my giver of wisdom; I am without eyesight and you kindle my vision.

TANSEN : Your Highness, you are so noble because of your humility. You are so much worshipped because of your magnanimity.

AKBAR	: Let the court be adjourned now. (*Approaching Katalu Khan*) Dear Katalu Khan, I have perhaps reassured you.
KATALU	: (*Aside*) Oh, Mukunda Dev! (*openly*) I beg your pardon, your Majesty. (*All are about to exit when a soldier enters from the opposite side.*)
SOLDIER	: Ruinous! Ruinous! (*All get up.*)
MANSINGH	: What's the news, soldier?
SOLDIER	: Suleman has rebelled.
MANSINGH	: Suleman!
AKBAR	: It's no wonder, King Mansingh. It was inevitable. I had anticipated it long ago.
KATALU	: I beg your pardon for my audacity. Isn't he the same Suleman who took refuge in you and you had magnanimously granted reprieve and restored his kingdom to him?
AKBAR	: I understand the implication of your question, Khan Saheb. You mean to say that Mukunda Dev may some day revolt.
KATALU	: Yes, your Majesty.
AKBAR	: Well! It is now time that Mukunda Dev was invited to put down the rebellion. Let his friendship be put to test.
KATALU	: (*aside*) Glory be to Allah, the Almighty!
AKBAR	: Katalu Khan, you too should proceed with several thousand soldiers to assist Mukunda Dev. I am convinced that Nawab Suleman has dared to revolt by relying on Kalapahad, his son-in-law.
KATALU	: It's certain. (*Aside*) Shall I play second fiddle to Mukunda Dev? Shall I be a subordinate to him? Well, I shall now show my mettle. (*Exit.*)

AKBAR	: Raja Saheb, make arrangements to send a messenger to Mukunda Dev immediately. Come, Mian Tansen. Come, dear Jester. (*Exit.*)
BIRBAL	: Let's go, your Majesty. Before mollification course ends, expedition to kill Kansa begins. Misfortune never comes alone. (*Exit.*)

(*Curtain*)

SCENE II

A Room in the Nine-storied Palace.
(*Mukunda Dev and the Queen are present.*)

MUKUNDA	: Darling! Aren't happiness after sorrow and union after separation gleeful?
QUEEN	: It's better than heavenly joys and sweeter than the enjoyment of nectar.
MUKUNDA	: Can this happiness be perpetual, dear?
QUEEN	: Why this inauspicious thought comes to your mind at this moment, dearest? Why do you upset me, My Lord?
MUKUNDA	: Dear, I have strange apprehensions. I don't know why?
QUEEN	: Apprehensions!!
MUKUNDA	: Every moment I feel - it rather rings in my ears - as if someone deeply hurts the inner recesses of my heart - I feel that human kind cannot bear so much happiness. - It is never eternal.
QUEEN	: Why is this sudden uncanny thought today, dear? Why is this poison of sudden sadness in the nectar of happiness? Why is

	this deep dark lining in the azure blue sky? Why is there a tinge of sin in this spotless heart? Oh, Lord of my heart! Oh, Lord of my life! (*embraces him*.)
MUKUNDA	: Oh, the goddess of my heart! Oh, the goddess of my soul! Calm down. It is a fleeting turmoil in my heart. It's a little anxiety.
QUEEN	: No, my Lord! You only assuage my fears. You are more firm than the Himalayas, more calm than the Pacific. Though fleeting, your presentiments may not be without a reason. It might be ominous like the premonitions of volcanic eruptions.
MUKUNDA	: Darling! Give up your fears. As the most powerful Emperor of Delhi has himself extended his friendship to us, as the Moghul army has tested the valour of Odisha in the battlefield and retreated, our fears are unfounded. Why should we worry?
QUEEN	: Can an enemy of yours put up with a heroic warrior like you?
MUKUNDA	: This predilection for fear is just. But Akbar… he is a jewel among the Moghuls. To worship humanity is his ideal. He recognises the worth of a warrior, whether he is a friend or a foe. He values the nobility of a noble soul. We needn't anticipate fear from him.
QUEEN	: Then….
MUKUNDA	: (*interrupting*) Darling, let's not continue

	with it. Look, how the setting sun is laughing and how beautiful the purple earth looks!
QUEEN	: How sweetly the travelling troubadours are singing!

(*A group of boys and girls enters while singing a chorus.*)
(Song)
Living an easeful life in a luxurious palace,
You needlessly look for joy and peace.
Life is only to do or shamelessly die,
Be selfless and never vie.
As you were born, you were ignorant,
Mother brought you up all with her heart,
It was her bliss and happiness,
That she gives up all her joys.
As you grew up older and wiser,
The world was still darker,
Father took care to make you grow wiser
Sacrificing all his joys for your own pleasure.
As you grew up still older,
Kinsmen, siblings grew fonder
Care for their wellbeing, dear,
Life can be better and nobler.
(*The royal couple are overwhelmed while listening to their song.*)

MUKUNDA	: (*Aside.*) How excellent the meaning of the song is! Action is the principal duty of a human being and self-sacrifice is his greatest pleasure.
QUEEN	: What makes you so thoughtful, dearest?
MUKUNDA	: Nothing, dear. I was just thinking that the song has nice meaning.
QUEEN	: Evening is approaching. Let's go. (*A maid-in-attendance enters.*)

Maid	: A messenger from Delhi has arrived and says that he is on an important errand.
QUEEN	: An important task! A messenger from Delhi! Dearest!
MUKUNDA	: Be calm, dear! There is nothing to be worried about. Action is our principal duty and self-sacrifice is our greatest pleasure. (*Exit.*)
QUEEN	: (*Aside.*) What is this new development? What is the reason of the sudden arrival of the messenger from Delhi? What misfortune follows! Will the king's premonitions come true? Will the joy of this great union end up in separation and sadness? Will the life in this nine-storied palace turn out to be the life in wilderness? Oh, my cruel God! Is it the happiness of the spouse of a warrior? (*A group of boys and girls again enters while singing a chorus, sing the same song again and exit. Mukunda Dev enters.*)
MUKUNDA	: Come, dear Queen. It's a day of great delight today. Bedeck me in the attire of a warrior.
QUEEN	: Oh, Lord of my life! My dearest! (*embraces*)
MUKUNDA	: Dearest! Are you so infirm being the wife of a warrior? Dear Queen! You are a heroic princess. Show up the grace of your heroism. Be proud of your intrepidness and exhort me with heroic words. Action is our principal duty and self-sacrifice is our greatest pleasure.
QUEEN	: Dearest! I know the time for love has

	come to an end. It is now time for duty. Well, there is nothing to fear. I am above all worries now. Please tell, my Lord, what's the news?
MUKUNDA	: Suleman, the Sultan of Bengal has rebelled. The emperor of Delhi has invited me to put down the rebellion.
QUEEN	: There is no need for delay. Days of luxury are over. It's now time for duty. Please, allow me, my Lord, to perform my duty as your queen at this critical time.
MUKUNDA	: (*embraces*) These are the right words of a real gallant queen. Action is the principal duty of a human being and self-sacrifice is his greatest pleasure. (*Exit.*)
	(*Curtain*)

SCENE III

The Conference Room in the Palace of Nawab Suleman.
(*Abdullah and Rahamat enter.*)

ABDULLAH	: Well, Commander! Am I not a warrior? Do I not know the art of warfare?
RAHAMAT	: You are the prince. If you are not a warrior, who else is? If you do not know how to fight, who else does? The other day you killed a mosquito with one blow. You cut your hand while killing a bird.
ABDULLAH	: That I had done long ago. Do you still remember it?
RAHAMAT	: Should I not remember it? If I should not remember such a glorious action of the prince, what should I remember then?

ABDULLAH : You marked how blood streamed from the cut in my hand. But did I care a little for it?

RAHAMAT : Why a little? Not at all. You completely closed your eyes and fainted.

ABDULLAH : Had he been anyone else he would have died at once.

RAHAMAT : He would not only have died but also have become a maimed ghost.

ABDULLAH : Then, why Commander? Why did my uncle give Dulia in marriage to a *Kafir*, when a warrior like me was available?

RAHAMAT : Don't you know, Prince, how women are tender; more so the princess? Hence, the Nawab perhaps thought that Dulia would not survive if she married a warrior like you.

ABDULLAH : (*gleefully*) You are right, Commander. Dulia is like an image of butter. But, Commander, why does Dulia call me a coward?

RAHAMAT : She wished she would marry you – perform *nikah* with you, so she tells it to you out of fun.

ABDULLAH : (*gleefully*) Does she call me a coward for fun. Let her do so. I am indeed a fool, a coward, a stupid, and silly. Well, Commander, Dulia loves me with all her heart. Why is she afraid to admit it openly?

RAHAMAT : Why wouldn't she? Will she not be afraid as long as that Kafir is there?

ABDULLAH : It's true. What is to be done now?

RAHAMAT : You have the means with you.

ABDULLAH	:	With me? Tell me what to do. I must do it. I can sacrifice my life for Dulia. Alas! Dulia!
RAHAMAT	:	Oh Prince, it's time for the Nawab to come. We shall discuss it later.
ABDULLAH	:	Dulia! Dulia! (*Exit.*)
RAHAMAT	:	This useless fellow is the means to my end. What humiliation! A Kafir will be the ruler of a Muslim kingdom. He will be the Commander of the Muslim army. – I am a perfect Muslim – a leading warrior – How can I be a subordinate worker – the slave of a mean Kafir? It is like death to a Muslim. Well, I have ignited a rebellion by all means. The rival to my ambition will either be ruined in the fire or come out with flying colours. But he can never live longer as Abdullah's sharp knife has been waiting for him with thirsty eyes. Let me see what happens.

(*The Nawab enters and Rahamat greets him.*)

NAWAB	:	Rahamat, is the rumour I hear true?
RAHAMAT	:	What rumour, Your Majesty?
NAWAB	:	You have masterminded this insurgency.
RAHAMAT	:	Yes, Your Majesty.
NAWAB	:	Did you consult Commander Kalapad about it?
RAHAMAT	:	Was it necessary, Your Majesty? Our soldiers, peasants, traders are not willing to accept the suzerainty of the Moghuls. May Your Highness give a little thought to it. Everybody wants that their motherland be free and Your Majesty shall remain her independent ruler. Isn't it natural?

NAWAB	: *(aside)* The intention is good. *(openly)* I too desire it. Do we have the strength to resist the most powerful Moghuls?
RAHAMAT	: Why not? Your Highness boasts that we can easily conquer the world under the commandership of Kalapahad.
NAWAB	: If he agrees, it is possible. But Commander Kalapahad does not seem to accord consent to this rebellion.
RAHAMAT	: *(aside)* Because he would not consent to it, I had to manipulate.
NAWAB	: What is your opinion, Rahamat? *(aside)* It is somewhat good that this insurgence has taken place. Who wants to lose freedom? But it's impossible to be successful without the help of Kalapahad. Won't he take part in it?

(Kalapahad enters.)

NAWAB	: Here is Kalapahad. What shall we do now?
KALAPAHAD	: Rahamat Ali knows what to do. Rahamat Ali, why, like an unwise person, did you cause this misfortune to happen? Do you know who you are revolting against? Where is the sea-like army of Moghuls and where is a pool-like army of Muslims? Where is the Moghul Emperor, the sovereign monarch of India; where is the Muslim Nawab of a small principality like Bengal? Is it possible to be victorious in this rebellion? Isn't it as impossible an action as drying up a sea by drinking up its water? Has the Nawab ever thought of how fatal its consequences will be?

RAHAMAT : How unheroic these words are from the mouth of a hero! How Kafir-like words these are on the part of a Muslim!

KALAPAHAD: These may be the words of a Kafir, Rahamat, but these are the words of a warrior. The Kafirs consider it an act of timidity to think of such a rebellion. Who do you obliquely call a 'Kafir'? Do you call them Kafirs, timid and uncivilised – the civilised Hindus who were once the beacon of the Aryan race, who illuminated the entire world with their wisdom?

NAWAB : Kalapahad!

KALAPAHAD: Sultan!

NAWAB : Who do you support?

KALAPAHAD: I speak in support of myself and my clan.

NAWAB : Is it your clan or the 'other'?

KALAPAHAD: (*aside*) The 'other'? To which clan do I then belong? Am I not a Hindu? Am I not a Brahmin? Isn't that hut my dwelling place? Do I not have an old mother? Do I not have a pious devoted woman as my wife?

(*Voice from the background*) : Yes, you have.

KALAPAHAD: Do they exist?

(*Voice from the background*) : Ha! Ha! Ha!

KALAPAHAD: Why this mocking laughter? Don't they exist? Are they dead? No. I am dead. I ... I ... Who is it then that feels?

NAWAB : Kalapahad!

KALAPAHAD: Kalapahad! Who is Kalapahad? I am Kalachand. – Don't you see that I am a Brahmin – wearing the sacred threads?

KALAPAHAD | 33

	– I pluck flowers everyday to worship God. – I live on vegetarian food. – All my activities are still of a Hindu. – Is it possible to change a name? My name is not Kalapahad. I am not a Muslim. I am a Hindu. I am Kalachand.
NAWAB	: Kalapahad, you are out your minds. Those are the things of your past.
KALAPAHAD:	Things of the past! Who am I now?
NAWAB	: You are a Muslim. You have courted the holy Islam. You are the son-in-law of the Nawab.
KALAPAHAD:	A follower of Islam! A Muslim! Son-in-law of the Nawab! – Not a Hindu? Hindu – (*Aside*) Oh! What recollections! – How cruel I am! – What a sinner! – What cruel deeds I have done out of selfish pride! – What are the means? What are the means? (*To the audience.*) Nawab, bid me farewell, please. My head is reeling. (*Exit Kalapahad.*)
NAWAB	: Rahamat, why is this transformation in Kalapahad? I don't understand him.
RAHAMAT	: Whether Your Highness understands him now or not, you have trusted him. You have made him your son-in-law, the Commander of your army. Now think of some ways to save the kingdom.
NAWAB	: Rahamat, you are the cause of this rebellion.
RAHAMAT	: I don't deny it, Your Highness.
NAWAB	: Who is responsible now?
RAHAMAT	: Your Highness, is it quite impossible to

	lead a battle without Kalapahad? Aren't we valiant? Aren't we warriors?
NAWAB	: I now declare you the Commander of my army. I am issuing the orders. (*Aside.*) But why is this change in Kalapahad? He might be ailing. The physician has to be called for to treat him immediately. Is it possible to win the war without him? He is everything for my dear Dulia and mine too. (*Exit.*)
RAHAMAT	: Bah! What fun! What fun! I am the Commander-in-chief. I am the Commander-in-chief. My enemy has gone mad. My enemy has gone mad. What if he recovers! No. I can never rest in peace as long as he is alive. (*Exit.*)

(*Curtain*)

SCENE IV
A Village Road.
(*Mukunda Dev enters with soldiers.*)

SOLDIERS	: Your Majesty! We are very hungry. Let orders be given so that we shall plunder people to collect food.
MUKUNDA	: Valiant soldiers! Is it gallantry?
1st SOLDIER	: Your Majesty! It is the land of our enemies.
MUKUNDA	: Of course, it is! But these villagers are not our enemies.
1st SOLDIER	: But the ruler of these people is our enemy.
MUKUNDA	: Is that why the innocent villagers are our enemies? - Ah! How painstaking are these villagers! - How hard they work

and take all care to supply food happily and selflessly to the kingdom and enrich the royal coffers! How generous at heart they are! They are never worried any day. What reward do they get for their industry? What do they gain in return? It's not all. When the kingdom faces war, as soon as the king urges them to join war, they wholeheartedly enter into the battle like insects flying into fire and sacrifice their lives. Can these honest subjects who are more than our life and children ever be hated? Can they ever be any one's enemies?

1st SOLDIER : Your Majesty! It is very hard to wait for food any longer.

MUKUNDA : You have, of course, waited for a long time. Do wait for a little more time. Let the messenger return.

(*The messenger along with some soldiers enters.*)

SOLDIERS : Your Majesty! The messenger has arrived. (*All the soldiers surround the messenger.*) Oh, messenger, please tell if you have any news. Are cartloads of food coming for us? (*The messenger keeps quiet.*)

SOLDIERS : Your Majesty!

MUKUNDA : I understand, messenger, we have been betrayed. (*aside*) What can we do now? (*to soldiers*) My dear soldiers, sell your horses, camels and elephants to collect food with the money you get in return.

SOLDIERS : (*Look at him with astonishment.*)

MUKUNDA : (*aside*) What can I do now? How can

	I manage the war? (*to soldiers*) Be off, soldiers.
	(*Soldiers are about to exit.*)
MUKUNDA	: Beware, Soldiers. The villagers should not be tortured by any means.
SOLDIERS	: As you wish, Your Majesty.
	(*Soldiers hurriedly exit.*)
MUKUNDA	: Didn't you get any sign of movement of our food carts, messenger?
MESSENGER	: Your Majesty, there is no doubt that the carts have started moving. The imprints of wheels can fairly be marked on the ground.
MUKUNDA	: Where did the carts go?
MESSENGER	: I followed the imprints and saw that they were clearly visible for half a mile approaching this direction.
MUKUNDA	: Then?
MESSENGER	: Then they disappeared into the jungle.
MUKUNDA	: Into the jungle? Have the foods been looted? Have the carts been misled or is it a trick of the enemy? Did you enter the jungle?
Messenger	: I didn't venture into the jungle because of darkness. I'll look into it on the morrow.
MUKUNDA	: (*aside*) We will make our both ends meet today in lieu of the horses etc. What shall we do tomorrow? How can we lead the battle? Why hasn't Katalu Khan arrived yet? He should have reached here by evening. (*A soldier enters.*)
SOLDIER	: A local Hindu landlord has supplied us food free, Your Majesty.

MUKUNDA : Free! Glory be to Lord Jagannath! Where is the gentleman?

SOLDIER : He is very old, Your Majesty. He is too weak to walk. He is making arrangements to welcome you.

MUKUNDA : So very kind! Let's go, soldiers, to visit him before our generous donor reaches us. Glory be to Lord Jagannath! How magnanimous you are! By your kindness, Katalu Khan must reach here in the mean time.

(*All exit. Katalu Khan enters from the opposite side.*)

KATALU : Why reaching? The man has reached. Bah! Bah! What fun! What a gift! Mukund, have an idea of Katalu's trick. What arrangements I have made for you to die from starvation! The cartloads of provisions have been captured by me. So, your life is in my hands. Now, let me see how you will survive and lead the battle; how you will receive the reward from the emperor for the victory. It is intolerable for a true Muslim to see that a Kafir is honoured in a court of the Muslims. Aren't we warriors? I shall show to the Badshah how imprudent Mukund Dev is; how he died for want of food ... and how clever, I, Katalu Khan, am! How I could put down the rebellion alone. Can I do it alone? If not by force, I shall try my cunning. First of all, I have to win Rahamat. I should not delay. (*Exit.*)

(*Curtain*)

SCENE V
Bed Chamber.
(Dulia is making a garland of flowers.)

FIROJA	:	Dulia, how beautiful you look in a silk saree with vermillion mark on your forehead, and bangles in hand!
DULIA	:	Do you mark, Dulia, of late he has been behaving like a Hindu.
FIROJA	:	Is that why you are putting on this attire?
DULIA	:	It's the noble duty of a wife to entertain the husband, Phiroza.
FIROJA	:	Dear friend, you really know what true love is, otherwise you would not have surrendered your youthful beauty fit for a Badshah to a Kafir.
DULIA	:	Don't say like that, Phiroza. It hurts. Love knows neither caste nor creed... neither wealth nor poverty ... neither a Kafir nor a Yaban.
FIROJA	:	Well, on his first appearance he was not so majestic. He looked lacklustre and jaded. He looked wild without proper apparel. What attracted him to you?
DULIA	:	Inner recesses of heart recognises the inner attraction.
FIROJA	:	Had it been my case, I wouldn't have glanced at him.
DULIA	:	Had it been the case now?
FIROJA	:	I would not have given him to you. Who will not be tempted by such a valiant warrior, a noble and wise person?
DULIA	:	Weren't these virtues conspicuous from his bearing during the first meeting?

FIROJA	:	A jeweller knows what a jewel is. How can a crow know that? Well, Dulia, you have a co-wife, don't you?
DULIA	:	Yes. Her name is Tilottama.
FIROJA	:	Does your husband love her still? Why should one adore a wild flower when he owns a rose?
DULIA	:	Oh, no. Tilottama is more devoted and beautiful than me. Oh, had we been together as twin sisters! But she is out and out a Hindu. However hard he tried, my husband could not convince her to give up her religion. My mother-in-law did not allow him to come near her. Alas, had I been with my mother-in-law, I could have attended on her!
FIROJA	:	I see, you have become an absolute Hindu, not only in dress and adornments but also in thinking.
DULIA	:	Look at the garland, Phiroza, I have made it fairly long. I don't feel well any longer.
FIROJA	:	How can you feel well? It is time for him to visit you. Let me go, I have a lot to attend. father's bed is yet to be made. (*Exit.*)
DULIA	:	(*holding the garland in her hand sings*)

(Song)
No other desire I have in me, darling,
Eternal love enchants my being
You are my Krishna and I am your Gopi,
Enter my heart with notes of your flute,
The melodious music pours like nectar,
I am yours for ever and ever.
(*Kalapahad enters.*)

KALAPAHAD: Go on singing, Dulia. What is that song? (*humming*) You are my Krishna and I am your Gopi, ...

DULIA : You are singing well.

KALAPAHAD: Is it as sweet and charming as yours?

DULIA : I feel so.

KALAPAHAD: It sounds good to you but it is no longer sweet to my ears.

DULIA : How do I bother if it is not so sweet to your ears?

KALAPAHAD: It is my song and you are singing it for my pleasure. How will it do if it is not sweet to me?

DULIA : Well, - I'll sing for your liking. Please be seated. Wear this garland.

KALAPAHAD: No. No. Give me my real garland. (*Kalapahad lets her clasp his neck with her hands.*)
(*Dulia sings the song again.*)

KALAPAHAD: Dulia, such love – such affection – can it be possible on the part of a female human? You are not a human - You are a goddess. Come, the deity of my heart, come my dear love, make me mad with your loving embrace and nectar-like sweet love. Let me forget that I was once a Hindu. I had a wife. I had my old mother. Now, I have lost my religion – lost my wife – lost my mother. But I have got endearment - care - affection and love. What bothers me then? What ails me now?

DULIA : Oh, Lord of my heart! Why do you torture me with pointless praise? What does this

	handmaid know about love? What does she know about endearment? This much I know that you are my husband – this handmaid is your worthless spouse. You are the lord of my heart - this maid is unfit to be your attendant.
KALAPAHAD:	What lofty thoughts! What profound love! What pure affection! Does it know the difference between a Hindu and a Muslim, a believer and a non-believer? Do you have such profound love for me, Tilottama? See, how nobler she is! Mother, do you have such unstinted affection? See, how deeper is Dulia's love for me! Come my beloved! Come, darling! Fill my heart with love and broaden my narrow mind. *(Embraces Dulia.)*
DULIA :	Oh, Lord of my heart! It is getting late in the night. You are not well too.
KALAPAHAD:	Dulia! Dulia! Oh, my dear Dulia! *(Embraces Dulia lovingly. Dulia helps him to bed and attends on him.)* Alas, why do I overlook such deep love and brood on doleful thoughts? *(Kalapahad falls asleep. Dulia exits. Tilottama enters as an apparition.)*
TILOTTAMA :	My Lord!
KALAPAHAD:	Who are you? Tilottama? Why have you come here? Have you changed your mind? Have you realised your mistake? Come and stay with me. You can stay as you like.
TILOTTAMA :	How do you repeat the same command,

	my lord? How can I change my religion? How, being a daughter, can I abandon my mother?
KALAPAHAD:	But, being a wife, you can desert your husband.
TILOTTAMA :	Can a Hindu wife do that, my lord? Does physical separation mean abandonment?
KALAPAHAD:	Whether it means that or not, take the example of Dulia. Try to understand once how she loves me. If I lead the life of a Hindu, she follows me as a Hindu. If I live as a Muslim, she too follows me as a Muslim. How natural and profound her love is! Do you have such love for me? Do you have such loving care for me?
TILOTTAMA :	Ha! Ha! Do you want to test my love and care for you? Well, look, I tear my heart open to you.
KALAPAHAD:	(*wondering*) What is it? What do I see?
TILOTTAMA :	(*laughing*) Did you see?
KALAPAHAD:	I saw, Tilottama; I saw.
TILOTTAMA :	What did you see?
KALAPAHAD:	My name - my figure - my thought.
TILOTTAMA :	Well, do I not have love for you? Do I not have loving care for you? Why are you surprised?
KALAPAHAD:	Why is one so bitter from outside when core of the heart is full of nectar?

(*Tilottama disappears. The apparition of the old mother appears.*)

MOTHER	: Won't she be bitter? Your taste is spoilt with the desire for lust. Debauched!
KALAPAHAD:	Debauched!
MOTHER	: Aren't you so? Would you surrender

yourself to the beauty of a woman if you had love for your wife, care for your mother, loyalty to your religion? Would you abandon us because of cool attraction of riches? Fie on your manhood! Fie on your learning! You have a lot to learn from this ignorant weak old woman. Alas! Who are you to me? My only son - the apple of my eye - the only prop to a blind person. But what has this frail, unwise woman done to you? I have sacrificed you on the alar of religion. I have forsaken you for the sake of society. You are nobody to me in this world. You are my enemy as for my duty. Look within; you can see your loving figure in my heart of hearts. Your sweet name is always on my lips.

KALAPAHAD: Mother! ... Mother!

MOTHER : See through the trap of illusion, through the pall of ignorance, you can realise what is real and what is unreal - what is nectar and what is poison.

(*The apparition of the old mother fades.*)

KALAPAHAD: (*getting up*) Where? Where are you, mother? No. no one is here. What did you pour into the ears of this sinner? What did you show to this blind son? I am indeed a debauch. I misunderstood lust for love and forgot my sense of duty. I studied the holy books, sincerely followed religion but I have deserted my wife. I have ignored my mother; neglected my religion, but how I can help it? What can do I to redeem

	myself? Let me return to my old mother, to my dutiful wife. I'll apologise with folded hands. I'll kneel down before them and apologise. No - no - how can I return to them? How can I return to them with this sinful face? I don't need this sinful life. (*Kalapahad covers his face.*) (*Abdullah enters with a knife in hand.*)
ABDULAH :	(*aside*) I need not delay. Dulia! - Dulia! See, I am not stupid today -. no longer timid - See, how clever I am! How valiant I am! (*attempts to stab Kalapahad*)
KALAPAHAD:	(*rising*) Come, Abdul, redeem me from this sinful life.
DULIA :	Oh, dear! (*shouting*) Who are you? (*Dulia grabs Abdullah's hand*) (*Curtain*)

ACT II
SCENE I
A Cottage.

(*Kalapahad's mother is lying on death bed. Tilottama is attending on her.*)

TILOTTAMA :	Ma! Please, be calm.
MOTHER :	(*excitedly*) Hear! Hear attentively! He had studied a lot – Everybody recognised him as a scholar - Everybody adored him as an earnest person. I got him married. My daughter-in-law is as beautiful as Goddess Laxmi, as learned as Goddess Saraswati and as chaste as Anasuya.
TILOTTAMA :	Ma! Why are you babbling? Please, try to sleep.

MOTHER : I was forbidding him. He was also not willing. People of the village persuaded him – Go to Nawab's court and appeal, so that you can get back your property. He went. What an unfortunate moment for him! He was trapped in the snares of a young witch and could not come back. My heart's treasure did not return. (*cries*)

(*Kalapahad enters.*)

KALAPAHAD: (*excitedly*) He did not return – How can he return? He is a Muslim.

TILOTTAMA : Who? – Who is there? Whose image is this? – Oh, Lord of my heart!

KALAPAHAD: (*approaching*) Stop there, devilish woman. Why this 'lord of my heart' again? Ha! – Ha! – Ha! – It's all in vain – futile labour.

TILOTTAMA : Oh, lord of my heart!

KALAPAHAD: Have you come again to capture me – clasp me in your delicate arms? – Grab me, – but this time Kalachand is not weak. Do you want to injure me – with your sidelong glance? – You may. – But now, Kalachand does not have a tender heart.

TILOTTAMA : Oh, lord of my life! I am your Tilottama.

KALAPAHAD: Tilottama! Darling Tilottama! Come. – Come. – No – No – don't touch me – I am an outcast. I have lost my Dharma. I have eaten forbidden foods. I have performed sacrilege. Don't touch me – Oh! don't touch me.

TILOTTAMA : (*tries to touch the figure but as she glances at the mother-in-law*) Ma! – Ma! Please,

	see, the treasure of your heart has indeed come back.
MOTHER	: Listen, dear! He has forsaken his Dharma. He has become a Musalman. He has taken beef. He has ruined both the worlds.
KALAPAHAD:	Certainly, I have ruined everything. I have taken beef and ruined everything. Who fed me? (*looking up*) Look, that demoness is laughing. She is laughing as she has fed me with forbidden foods. She is dancing and clapping because she has converted me. Look, she is running towards me – with her mouth open – to devour me – to eat me up – Ma! – Ma! – hold me – hide me. (*moves to embrace mother*)
MOTHER	: Don't touch me. – Don't touch me. Don't make me an outcast with your touch – (*addressing Tilottama*) Ma! – Ma! – Come closer to me. Come to my lap – he'll touch you – he'll touch you.
TILOTTAMA :	(*aside*) Oh, society! How strong is your hold on us! For your sake, a son is unable to touch his mother. A wife cannot touch her husband.
KALAPAHAD:	Ma! – Ma! – that demoness is still chasing me. Save your Kala, Ma! Save your Chand.
MOTHER	: (*getting up*) What did you say? What did I hear? Tell me again. Are you Kalachand, a jewel tied to the end of my saree – the apple of my eye – the prop of this blind old woman? No. You are a cheat – a liar. My Kalachand is dead long since. Kalachand does no longer belong to this world.

	Alas, Kalachand! The support of this old woman! – The saviour of the weak woman! – The last refuge of the poor! Where are you, dear son? - Come to me, dear.
KALAPAHAD:	Dead - Kalachand is dead – for torturing his wife – for tormenting his mother. - I couldn't hold him for a little more time. I couldn't punish him before seeing him off. He died – he cheated all.
TILOTTAMA :	Oh, lord of my life! What a heart-rending scene! Mother is insane – the husband is insane too – the whole world is mad. - What is the need of this life in this mad bad world? Oh, Bajra, the weapon of Lord Indra! Haven't you lost your mind? Oh Sea! Haven't you lost your mind? Be mad – dance in madness without delay – roar in madness without delay. Release my maddened soul from the bondage of flesh. (*collapses*)
KALAPAHAD:	(*Addressing Tilottama*) Who are you? Who are you? Ma, it is the same demoness. She has come again. I am frightened, Ma. Take me to your lap - hold me in your arms.
MOTHER :	(*running at him*) I'll take you into my lap, dear, – hold you in my arms. You needn't fear, son. - Eh, who are you? Are you Kalachand? No, you are not my Kalachand. You are a Muslim. You are Kalapahad. (*She rises up and sits on her bed.*)
KALAPAHAD:	Kalapahad! Kalapahad! He died that day. - I have buried him myself. Mother, I am Kalachand. I am not Kalapahad. I am a

	Hindu, not a Musalman.
MOTHER	: Aren't you a Musalman? A Hindu! Can you become a Hindu?
KALAPAHAD:	I have not yet become a Hindu. I shall be a Hindu. Ma, I shall be a Hindu. Can't I be a Hindu, Ma?
MOTHER	: Why can't you be, son? Cry, - only cry, - all your sins will be washed away with your tears. You will be redeemed of all your sins. Go to Lord Jagannath at Neelachal, the saviour of the poor, redeemer of all sins. Touch his lotus feet; concentrate on His holy name; surrender your body, mind and life to Him. - He shall bless you and you will have redemption.
KALAPAHAD:	I shall certainly be blessed - I shall certainly be redeemed - Bah! Bah! Then I shall cry, – cry my heart out. I shall go to Neelachal – I will proceed just now. I'll embrace Lord Jagannath and say with all one mind, with all concentration, "My mother has sent me to you. Bless me. Redeem me. Make me a Hindu." But, Mother, will you take me in your arms on my return?
MOTHER	: Shall I not take you in my arms? - Shall I not take my son in my arms? What else shall I do in this world then? What shall I do in this life, son? Where are you now, my son? Where are you now, leaving your old mother and pious wife? Show up once and make my eyes glorified. Speak a few words to me, so that my ears will

be consecrated. Touch me once, so that my life will be calm. How can he do it? Will he ever come? Does he exist? Is he alive? I am alive; he is not. Uh! He is not alive. Daughter-in-law, Daughter-in-law! He is not alive. Ka-la-chand. (*dies*)

TILOTTAMA : Ma! Ma! – what has happened to you? Why have you closed your eyes?

KALAPAHAD: Fall asleep, Ma! Sleep without worries. I am leaving just now. I shall get the boon from Lord Jagannath. I shall be a Hindu. You will take me into your arms. Bah! Bah! Mothe will take me in her arms. (*exit*)

TILOTTAMA : Oh, lord of my heart! Where are you going - leaving this wretch alone in sorrow? (*collapses*)

(*Dulia and Firoja enter.*)

DULIA : Oh, lord of my life! Where is he, Firoja? Please tell, "Where is the lord of my life?" This is the same hut. Oh, lord of my life! (*collapses*)

FIROJA : Be calm, dear.

TILOTTAMA : Who is this mad woman?

FIROJA : Oh, chaste woman! Are you Tilottama?

TILOTTAMA : Yes, this wretched woman's name is Tilottama.

DULIA : (*getting up*) Tilottama! Sister, where is he? Where is he, sister? Please, show him to me, sister. Please, show him to me at once.

TILOTTAMA : (*aside*) Is she that same fortunate woman? Is she a Muslim? How insane she is in the absence of the husband!

DULIA : Sister, why are you silent? Do you think

| | that I have come to snatch the lord of your life from you? I have come only to have a glance at him. I have come just to have some dust from his feet. Show him to me once, sister. Bring him to me once, sister. Oh, lord of my life! Please be kind to this poor miserable woman, lord. In your absence all the world before me is lost in darkness. I am not at peace with myself. |

TILOTTAMA : Sister! Sister! You are indeed my sister. You are not a Musalman; you are a Hindu. You are a devoted wife. You are a virtuous woman. Oh, society! I wish you were not so stringent. Oh, Dharma! If I were not afraid of you, I would forget the difference between a Hindu and a Musalman - I would forget the difference between Allah and God and embrace this chaste lady. I would make my life glorified - make my life meaningful.

DULIA : Can I be so fortunate, sister, - can I enjoy embracing a goddess-like sister as you? Well, leave it. Please tell, sister, "Where is the lord of my life?" Please, go in and call him. What is this scene? What do I see, sister?

TILOTTAMA : Mother is no more, sister. Now, our husband is at Neelachal and the mother-in-law is in heaven.

DULIA : Mother is no more! Isn't mother-in-law in this world? Alas! How cruel I was that you had to suffer so much because of me, mother! Had I seen you alive once, I

	would have begged your forgiveness and consecrated my ears by listening to you addressing me as "daughter-in-law." Uh! How sad! What a suffering! Now, our husband is at Neelachal and the mother-in-law is in heaven. We, two hapless women, are left behind. Go back, Firoza. I won't stay here any longer. I will follow my husband. If I don't find him, I will follow my mother-in-law. Farewell. (*Exit.*)
FIROJA	: Darling! - Darling! (*Exit.*)
TILOTTAMA	: Sister! What an example of devotion to husband you show! What an example of love for husband! Go, sister! Go without any obstacle. I wish you would soon meet him. Bless him, mother. Let wishes of our husband be fulfilled. I wish I would soon gladly follow you.

(*Sits down on the bed.*)
(*Curtain*)

SCENE II
A camp in the battle field.

(*Nawab Suleman and a messenger enter.*)

SULEMAN	: Tell, messenger, did you get any news?
MESSENGER	: I have told you, Your Highness, that there is no news.
SULEMAN	: Impossible! Continue the search. My Dulia is absent. Kalapahad is absent too. It is impossible! (*"Hail, Mukunda Dev! Hail, Mukunda Dev!" is heard from the background.*)

SULEMAN	:	What is this loud cheering for? (*Another messenger enters.*)
2nd MESSENGER	:	Your Highness, Mukunda Dev has invaded the camp.
SULEMAN	:	Where is our commander? Where are our soldiers?
2nd MESSENGER	:	There is no one here. I don't see anyone. You can see, Your Highness, the enemy soldiers are approaching. Please, listen to their cheerful sounds of "Jai". (*Shouts of "Hail, Lord Jagannath! Hail, Mukunda Dev!" are heard from the background.*)
SULEMAN	:	What a crisis! Where is Rahamat? He told me that he would wait at the hill pass to attack the enemy soldiers. Isn't he there? Is he defeated or has he deserted? What a conspiracy! Now, the enemy soldiers are running towards me. My bodyguards are also not here. Call for a sword for me, messenger. (*Messenger exits. Suleman anxiously gazes at the horizon.*)
MESSENGER	:	Undone! Undone! Nobody is around … not a weapon is available.
SULEMAN	:	Nobody is around! Not a weapon is available! What a severe conspiracy! Oh, Kalapahad! Oh, Kalapahad! What a blunder I have done by relying on Rahamat Ali! Can't I see you at this final moment, Dulia? Abdul – (*Soldiers from Utkal enter.*)
SOLDIERS	:	Here is the Nawab. Attack him.
SULEMAN	:	A sword! … A sword!

SOLDIERS	:	Hack him. It is a golden opportunity. (*Soldiers are ready to attack the Nawab. Mukunda Dev enters.*)
MUKUNDA	:	Beware, soldiers! The enemy is alone and without weapons. Can't you see it? Are you Kshatriyas or Chandals? Please come, Nawab Saheb - excuse us - take this sword - (*Gives the Nawab a sword.*) - defend yourself.
SULEMAN	:	Who are you, oh, magnanimous warrior? Are you Mukunda Dev? How noble you are!
MUKUNDA	:	There is nothing to be surprised about, Nawab Saheb. This is the rudimentary principle of a Kshatriya in the battle field.
SULEMAN	:	But I am alone.
MUKUNDA	:	You need not fear, Nawab Saheb. I am your only opponent. As long as we are engaged in a duel, my soldiers will not advance an inch towards you.
SULEMAN	:	What a generous soul!
MUKUNDA	:	Dear Nawab Saheb, don't indulge in needless praise. You are a warrior, fight like one. A true warrior does not procrastinate with pointless praise.
SULEMAN	:	Certainly. I am a warrior and I'll fight like a warrior.
MUKUNDA	:	I am ready. (*Suleman collapses while fighting.*)
SOLDIERS	:	"Hail, Mukunda Dev! Hail, Mughal Emperor Akbar!"
MUKUNDA	:	Soldiers, arrest the Nawab and bring him to my camp. (*aside*) What treachery!

	How treacherous Katalu and Rahamat are! Fortunately, the secret letter was intercepted by us otherwise we would have been doomed. They might be scheming to make a combined attack on us. Let me not delay. I have a handful of soldiers. I should be careful. (*Exit.*)
SULEMAN	: Alas! Why didn't you kill me? I have lost my Dulia … I have lost my Kalapahad. The goddess of victory is not pleased with me. I no longer enjoy peace and happiness. Why should I have this life? Oh, Rahamat! If I catch sight of you once, if I have you off guard, I shall smash your head with a blow of this fist. Why this vain thought? Why this vain hope? All depends on Allah, the Almighty. Soldiers, take me wherever you like. (*exit as a prisoner*)

(*Katalu and Rahamat enter.*)

KATALU	: Mr. Ali, the hurdle for you is overcome. What do you plan for getting rid of my obstacle?
RAHAMAT	: I had a beautiful plan - it was spoiled by a whisker. Had the secret letter not reached Mukunda Dev, they would have all died of hunger, and the Nawab imprisoned by us. But Mukunda Dev has taken him as a prisoner.
KATALU	: What did you write in the letter?
RAHAMAT	: How I have hidden the carts of food that you have stolen from him, what arrangements I have made to combine my army with yours, and how I have won

	the confidence of the Nawab and left him alone in the camp ...
KATALU	: Who did you send the letter by?
RAHAMAT	: By Abdul - he is so stupid - he mistook Mukunda as you and delivered the letter to him.
KATALU	: What a blunder! Well, leave it. What shall we do now?
RAHAMAT	: Assassination!
KATALU	: But who will do it?
RAHAMAT	: Abdul. (*Abdul enters.*)
ABDUL	: Here I am, guys. Where is Dulia, Commander? You told me to hand over Dulia to me after I had delivered your letter. Where is she? Where is my darling.
KATALU	: Is he your friend, the messenger?
RAHAMAT	: I have thought of doing the assassination by him.
KATALU	: Again, by this fool? Let him not finish you this time instead of Mukunda Deb.
RAHAMAT	: There is no need to fear now. Now he recognises him well. Look, prince, if you can do one more task, you shall definitely get Dulia.
ABDUL	: No, no, commander, I shall not listen to you any longer. I shall not do your job again. Dear Dulia – My life – My darling!
RAHAMAT	: This time before this gentleman as the witness, I swear that you must get Dulia if you do one more job.
ABDUL	: Must I get my darling? Tell me about the assignment. Be quick. Oh, my Dulia!
RAHAMAT	: Take this knife. Assassinate the man

		you have handed over the secret letter earlier.
RAHAMAT	:	Eh, assassination again, commander! The last assassination comes to my mind. How I got caught! Had my uncle come to know about it - fortunately -
RAHAMAT	:	Well, see you. Forget Dulia. I don't care for anything, commander.
ABDUL	:	How should I forget Dulia? Give me the knife. I shall finish him just now. - but -
RAHAMAT	:	Again 'but' - well, Dulia -
ABDUL	:	No, commander - I have no fear - but will you surely give Dulia to me?
RAHAMAT	:	Definitely. But you have to be very careful this time. Take care that you are not caught like the last instance.
ABDUL	:	(*taking the knife from Rahamat*) You need not fear I can do this work with much ease. Look, he has given me this ring and told me that if I show it to his soldiers, they will never detain me.
KATALU	:	Bah! Bah! What a gift! How interesting!
ABDUL	:	But will you give Dulia to me?
RAHAMAT	:	How many times shall I assure you?
ABDUL	:	Then I am ready to go. Dear Dulia – my life –. My darling! But one more thing, commander.
RAHAMAT	:	What?
ABDUL	:	Making us Badshah and Begum – Will you fulfil that?
RAHAMAT	:	How many times shall I assure you? Finish the job first.
ABDUL	:	Bah! Dulia shall be Begum and I shall be

	the Badshah. Won't it be so, commander? Dulia shall be Badshah – I shall be the Begum.
RAHAMAT	: It shall be so.
ABDUL	: I take leave of you. Dulia – Dulia – (*Exit.*)
KATALU	: You have arranged a good mad fellow.
RAHAMAT	: I have spurred his madness. You can see how useful he is.
KATALU	: See Rahamat, I shall never leave Mukunda Deb alive. If he survives Badshah will come to know everything. You can surmise my predicament.
ABDUL	: You needn't worry. Abdul will do the job cleanly. Khan Saheb, how miserable Nawab is now!
KATALU	: Do you feel bad for him, Ali Saheb? But when you are on your throne, the court is agog with dancers and wine, will you be sorry then?
RAHAMAT	: I shall feel sorry if the Nawab is alive.
KATALU	: You have rightly spoken what is in my mind, dear. Come dear friend, let's embrace each other and cement our friendship.

(*Curtain*)

SCENE III
Fort Barabati.

(*Shikhi and Manai enter.*)

| SHIKHI | : What pitch darkness, brother! I have never seen such a dark rainy night in my life. |
| MANAI | : It has also started drizzling. |

SHIKHI	: Uh, how dark it is! It is so late in the night. Why isn't he returning?
MANAI	: Why are you so restless? It is not so late in the night. I guess it is only the first hour of the night.
SHIKHI	: But see, how dark it is! How silent it is! It seems as if it is midnight.
MANAI	: Do you realise, brother? It is perhaps the will of God, or else we would not have got such a chance.
SHIKHI	: Is there any doubt in it? It seems as if this darkness is ordained for him.
MANAI	: Remember, brother, if you are the commander, you should not be as arrogant as he.
SHIKHI	: Why do you say so, brother? It is not untrue that we are going to do it only for our king.
MANAI	: Oh, yes. It is so. We could have tolerated if someone from outside had been introduced into that position. How can we tolerate if we are superseded by such a junior fellow?
SHIKHI	: How humiliating! Is he better informed or more learned than us? He has only the gift of the gab. He has only a glib tongue, nothing more. What kind of dexterity did he show in this battle?
MANAI	: What to speak of his heroism? When the old commander fell, he bravely gathered all the soldiers and marched towards the battle field. We, sons of the soil, returned to our homes.

SHIKHI	: As we returned, we were saved. A number of soldiers did like us and saved themselves. He lost all his men in the battle. He too was severely wounded. We very well realise how the king was benefited by it but the king does not realise it. He said that we were timid - timorous - he is courageous - valiant - so he made him the commander.
MANAI	: Now, the brave one has gone. Let's see whether he returns or not.
SHIKHI	: Won't he return?
MANAI	: Eh! Be quiet. There is some noise. Has he returned? Let's stand away.
SHIKHI	: Why? Let's finish him at once. (*Dulia enters.*)
DULIA	: Uh, how dark it is! (*Shikhi stabs her and they exit.*)
DULIA	: Uh, (*collapses*). I'm dying, Firoja. Oh, the lord of my life, I'm dying! (*Firoja and Golap enter.*)
PHIROJA	: Who are you, dear boy? You have a good name. How could you recognise Dulia?
GOLAP	: I belong to Bengal. Should I not recognise the daughter of the Nawab?
PHIROJA	: Had we stayed a few days more in this inn, she could have completely recovered. But she did not pay heed to us. As soon as she had strength enough to walk, she started off without caring for the darkness of the night nor for the rough roads. I pointed out to her that we are women, and we should not set out at night and

	wait for the morning, she did not care for me. Now, see, she has left me alone and is walking off. - Well, are you coming with us? It would be fine if you came with us. You will be of great help.
GOLAP	: I am also going to visit Lord Jagannath. But it is so dark now - and I hear robbers prowl on the way -
PHIROJA	: Therefore, I am looking for a boy companion.
GOLAP	: How surprising! You are the Nawab's kinsmen – moreover you are ladies – how have you set out on a journey alone?
PHIROJA	: (*aside*) People behave like this if they are in love. How can you understand it? (*to the boy*) that's a long story.
GOLAP	: Well, as you are the kinsmen of our Nawab and requesting me to accompany you, I shall go with you, come what may.
PHIROJA	: Hurry up, brother, my friend has gone away somewhere like a mad woman.
DULIA	: Oh, lord of my life! –
GOLAP	: Who is crying?
PHIROJA	: It seems to be the tone of my friend.
DULIA	: Give me a little water, Firoja. A little water –
PHIROJA	: Dear friend, what is the matter with you? (*embraces Dulia*) What is this? Are you bleeding, dear?
GOLAP	: Blood! Light please – light please. (*The commander enters with a torch.*)
COMMANDER:	Who needs light, traveller?
GOLAP	: Where – Where is blood?

PHIROJA	:	Flowing from her hand.
GOLAP	:	Jai Jagannath! Bandage the wound with this piece of cloth. (*Tears a piece of cloth from his turban.*)
DULIA	:	Give me a little water – I feel very thirsty.
COMMANDER	:	I am getting you some water. (*aside*) Who has done this brutality? Even in front of the fort? (*The commander opens the gate of the fort and exits.*)
PHIROJA	:	Dear friend, please speak a little. Can my friend survive, Golap?
GOLAP	:	You needn't fear. Thank God, the knife has missed its target.
DULIA	:	Oh, lord of my life! - Give me a little water, Firoja. I am very thirsty.
GOLAP	:	(*sighs.*) Is she a human or a goddess? What profound love! (*The Queen and the Commander enter.*)
COMMANDER	:	Honourable Queen, why do you take the pains to come out?
QUEEN	:	Why Commander? Is there any harm in it? - A woman is stabbed - that too in front of the fort! How surprising! Shouldn't the king look into the matter? Should I not take care of her in his absence? Tell Commander, where is the girl?
DULIA	:	Uh, I am dying. Water – water –
QUEEN	:	(*coming closer*) Have some water. (*makes Dulia drink water*) Commander, please call for the maids immediately. Let's take her into the fort and attend to her. (*Commander exits.*)

DULIA	:	Mother, you are a Hindu.
QUEEN	:	Why? Is there any –
DULIA	:	I am a Muslim, Mother.
QUEEN	:	Why should you make a distinction between a Hindu and a Muslim at this time?
DULIA	:	I also belong to your enemy kingdom, Mother. -
QUEEN	:	Why do you fear? It's the duty of a Kshatriya to rescue a person in danger. It is also the duty of a Kshatriya to give shelter to the destitute. There is no question of caste or creed - believer or non-believer - friend or foe.
DULIA	:	How magnanimous is a Kshatriya's heart! I have regained my strength a little. I thank you from the core of my heart. Firoja, thank the saviour and let's go. I can't tolerate any more delay - Oh, the lord of my life! When can I meet you? (*about to leave*)
QUEEN	:	How is it? Where will you go at this hour of the night? Has your husband deserted you?
PHIROJA	:	Mother, it's a long story.
QUEEN	:	Any way, I won't leave you alone at this hour. It appears from your demeanour that you belong to an aristocratic family. Some misfortune must have befallen you. Therefore, I won't let you go unless I do something needful for you. Moreover, cruelty has been meted out to an alien in front of my fort. - Tell me how I can allow you, a person in danger, to leave without thorough investigation and without proper

action. What would my subjects say? What would the neighbouring kings say? What would my conscience say? - the kingdom of Lord Jagannath a sinful kingdom – there is anarchy during Mukunda Dev's reign.

DULIA : Oh, the lord of my life! Here - I'm coming. Come Firoja, I can't wait any longer.

GOLAP : (*aside*) Are you a human or a goddess, Dulia? I feel like touching your feet.

QUEEN : (*aside*) She is as miserable as I am. Oh God! Why did You create separation along with union? - Why did You create sorrow along with happiness?

DULIA : Please allow us to take your leave, mother.

QUEEN : Impossible. I request you to be my guest tonight. Here, my maids have come.
(*Commander along with the maids enters.*)

DULIA : I cannot ignore my saviour's request when she insists.

QUEEN : Dear Commander, this boy is your responsibility.

DULIA : Please, see us off as soon as it is morning tomorrow.

QUEEN : It's tomorrow's matter. Please allow me to entertain you as my guest for this night.

DULIA : Are you a human or a goddess, Mother?

QUEEN : There is nothing to be praised about. It is my general duty. Maids, help her to come inside.
(*Maids try to support Dulia.*)

DULIA : It's not necessary. I don't feel any pain. I can very well walk. (*All enter the fortress.*)
(*Curtain*)

SCENE IV

Battle field. Mukunda Deb's Camp.
(*Mukunda Deb and Suleman enter.*)

MUKUNDA : Nawab Saheb, I have understood everything from Rahamat's letter. It is a great conspiracy. Their clandestine motive is to deprive you of your kingdom by murdering you by your enemies and deprive me of my life and honour. You are now completely aware of it.

SULEMAN : What should we do now?

MUKUNDA : You need not worry about yourself. As long as I am alive, your kingdom is safe. I have already written a letter to the Emperor Akbar about the terms of truce and the treachery of Katalu Khan. We have to wait here till we receive his reply.

SULEMAN : But you have to be very careful because the combined army of the Moghuls and the Muslims is larger than yours.

MUKUNDA : The number does not matter. However small, when the army realises that it is engaged in a righteous war, it can do what a large number of soldiers cannot do. But I know very well about Katalu's schemes. I also learnt all about Rahamat's schemes from you. So, I am not worried about them. It is very late in the night. Please take rest.

SULEMAN : Aren't you going to take rest?

MUKUNDA : You needn't worry about me, please. (*about to leave*)

SULEMAN : Let me put out the light.

MUKUNDA	:	If you so feel like, you can put it out, but it is very much necessary.
SULEMAN	:	Good night, King.
MUKUNDA	:	Good night, Nawab Saheb. (*Mukunda Deb goes out.*)
SULEMAN	:	Man's destiny changes like this. Sometimes he is on his throne - on the apex of happiness - sometimes on a bed of grass - in the abyss of misery. Strange! A metamorphosis - beyond thoughts - beyond dreams! Man proposes but God disposes. How I thought of winning the battle - Be an independent Nawab - enjoying my reign over a free kingdom, and what happened in reality? I'm defeated - imprisoned - a captive - not even the owner of a grass bed. Alas, what a pathetic transformation! I am mystified. Dulia! - Dulia! - Where are you, my dear? Kalapahad - Kalapahad - where did you disappear? Why did you leave us? Did you desert me angrily as I did not follow your counsel? Had you been here, had I listened to your advice, could the scoundrel and devilish Rahamat have done such a damage to me? - Would the Nawab of Bengal have been compelled to sleep on the ground as a prisoner? Uh! My head reels to think of anything. (*Nawab falls asleep and Abdul enters.*)
ABDUL	:	Oh, this is the room of Mukunda Deb. How dark it is! Where is he sleeping? Dulia, that day you called me a killer and kicked me out. See, how the commander has confined

you to the prison to give you in marriage to me. It is fine that uncle has been taken as a prisoner. Why am I anxiety-ridden? Rahamat has told me that I shall be the Nawab and Dulia will be my queen - No. Dulia will be my Badshah and I shall be her Begum. I mean Dulia will command me as a Badshah and I shall obey her as a Begum. Bah - Bah, what fun! Bring, Siraji. Wait, let me finish the job. Where? - Where is he sleeping? - Here, he is snoring loudly. (*Abdul stabs the sleeping Nawab in the chest.*)

SULEMAN : Uh! I'm dying. I'm dying.
ABDUL : Who are you? Whose tone is this?
SULEMAN : Uh, Dulia!
ABDUL : Who are you? Uncle?
SULEMAN : Who are you? Whose tone is this? - Abdul?
ABDUL : Uncle! What did I do? (*embraces the Nawab*)
SULEMAN : Abdul! Abdul! (*embracing him*) You have done the right thing. I know you have come to murder Mukunda Deb. You have done the right thing. My dream has come true. I have been redeemed of my sins. Listen, son, the tale of my sins. Let me die peacefully.
ABDUL : Uncle – Uncle –
SULEMAN : My strength is declining. You are the only son of my elder brother and Dulia is his only daughter. My brother died young. I became your guardian. I made you a dunce because of my greed for the kingdom. When you are of age, I declared that you are insane. My wishes were fulfilled. As

KALAPAHAD | 67

	I brought up Dulia as my daughter, she considered me her father. You also had the same feeling.
ABDUL	: Is Dulia my sister, uncle? Oh, what a sinner I am! Rahamat ….
SULEMAN	: I understand, son, you have come do it on the instigation of Rahamat. Beware, he is a traitor. Don't trust him any longer. I advise you to look for Kalapahad and Dulia. Rescue your kingdom.
ABDUL	: Uncle – Uncle - uh, what a heinous deed I have done! Rahamat, I'll show you how devilish I am … what a great killer I am! Dulia, my sister, forgive me. Uncle, forgive this useless son of yours.
SULEMAN	: My son, you need not beg apology. It's a Divine punishment. It is redemption of my sins. You are not at fault. I am free now. It's only for you that I am free from the burden of my sins. Dulia – Dulia - Kalapahad - Kalapahad, it's a great regret that I could not see you at the final moments. However, I am happy that Abdul has returned to my bosom. Abdul, I have not showed you my affection as long as I lived. Now, at the death's door, let me be content to embrace you and cool my soul. (*embraces Abdul*) Abdul - Kalapahad. (*dies*)
ABDUL	: Uncle – Uncle - don't leave me alone. Go to that immortal world - shine among the stars as a brilliant star. Let me receive a ray of light from that shining star - a streak of strength from that perpetual source of

energy and proceed on the path of life. Let me absorb myself on my destined path of duty. Rahamat - Rahamat - you devil! (*Exit.*)
(*Mukunda Deb hastily enters.*)

MUKUNDA : Please, get up, Nawab Saheb. (*aside*) As what I have seen, it is not desirable to stay here any longer. The combined army of the Mughals and Muslims is thrice the size of mine. Moreover, the traitors have spread the rumours that I am a Kafir and I have come to rule over the Muslims. Therefore, there is no doubt that they will fight with greater enthusiasm. In this situation there will be a great loss of lives for me and nothing else. I have to go to Delhi myself. I shall relate everything to the Emperor and bring more soldiers. (*loudly*) Please, get up, Nawab Saheb. (*looking at the bed*) What is it? Where is Nawab Saheb? Where is the prisoner? Has the prisoner escaped? Guard!

(*Guard enters.*)

GUARD : (*while wiping his eyes*) Your Highness!
MUKUNDA : Where is the prisoner?
GUARD : Prisoner? (*looking at the bed*) He - re. (*aside*) Where is the prisoner? (*to the king*) Your Highness!
MUKUNDA : Where is the prisoner?
GUARD : I beg your pardon, Your Highness! This humble servant was resting for a while due to tiredness.
MUKUNDA : What did you say? Did you sleep due to

tiredness? 'Tiredness' from the mouth of an Odia soldier! How could you utter 'sleeping'? Is it the same Odia race whose physical prowess has kept this vast Odia tract safe from the ever-hungry invincible power of the Mughals? Is it the same Odia race in whose veins the hot blood of the Kesharis and Gangas is still flowing? Then, what is this state of affairs? What kind of glory of the race is being displayed now before its own conscience, - before other races - before the whole world? Sleeping during the time of remaining awake! - Sluggishness at the time of duty! - Dreariness at the time war! What a fall! What a downfall of the descendants of the Kesharis and Gangas! Oh, stars! What did you show me today under your luminous light? Oh, winds! What sounds did your strong waves bring to my ears? Weariness of an Odia! Sleep for an Odia! Has the glory of the ancestors come to an end today? Has the traditional reverence for the mother come to an end today? What do I hear? What do I behold? What is this horrible sight appearing in the brow of the sky? What is this wailing sound floating in the wind? The racial superiority of the Odias is submerged in the abysmal depth of the sea at Neelachal! Freedom of the Odias is torn into smithereens like the stone slab at Dasaswamedha Ghat!

(*Voices of soldiers is heard from the background.*)

Soldiers	:	Your Majesty! Your Majesty!
MUKUNDA	:	Arise, Mukunda Deb! Protect the glory and freedom of Odisha till your last breath.

(Exit hastily.)
(Curtain)

SCENE V
In front of the Temple of Lord Jagannath.
(Kalapahad and the Pundits enter.)

KALAPAHAD: Oh, Lord! My Great Lord! How long will you take to shower mercy on this sinner? My blood has dried up by constant prayer - Light has faded from my heart - I am unable to call you any more, My Lord. Please appear before me, oh, Redeemer of the Downtrodden. Oh, Lord of the poor, please, have mercy on this poor soul.

PUNDIT I : Arey infidel! Why are you hanging out here in vain? This is not a mosque or a church to amalgamate all castes and creeds.

KALAPAHAD: Honourable ones, I was a Hindu. Lord Chaitanya once converted an infidel into a Hindu.

PUNDIT II : Why are you citing the example of Lord Chaitanya? Was he a family man like us? - He was a free soul. - Did he ever care whether you are a Christian or a Muslim? He never cared for any caste. Look, the members of *Mukti Mandap* are not anybody's bonded labour so that they will assemble in a committee and decide an issue without fees. Donate something. - Empty your purse. You don't belong to the have-nots.

KALAPAHAD: Oh, my Lord, what do I hear? Why do you tarnish these sinful ears? Why do you scandalise the holy Hindu religion?

PUNDIT II : What a religious person! Let's go away from here. Shall we get anything by hanging out here? If we had sat on the *Mandap*, we would have earned a few coins.

PUNDIT I : Look, infidel! You needn't wait around here. If one gives up his religion once, he has no right to court it again.

KALAPAHAD: How cruel the religion is! No, sirs, please consider my case once again with a simple heart. This sinner swears, swears in the name of Lord Jagannath that this humble slave is adequately repentant. This sinner is ready to accept any punishment meted out to him for his sins. Please consider my case favourably. Please excuse me once so that I can once again attend on my ailing mother, and this unfortunate being can embrace his virtuous wife.

PUNDIT II : Come, let's go. Why do you listen to his discourse? Will this shameless person pay anything to us to listen to him?

KALAPAHAD: Aren't you a pundit? Is it the desirable conduct of a pundit?

PUNDIT II : (*sneering*) Eh, listen to him. He is a pundit! Oh, shameless fellow! Aren't we pundits?

	Are you a pundit? Place some money here, offer some gold coins, you can see whether scholasticism comes out or not; whether we are bringing out the right rituals for atonement from the scripture or not.
KALAPAHAD:	Does justice depend on bribe not on conscience? Do the rituals for atonement depend on money not on repentance? Is this Hinduism? - Is it the same ancient Hinduism that is rich in various scriptures and glorified by several incarnations? Is this the final outcome? Impossible! - Impossible! Oh, my Lord! Please, put an end to this test - Have mercy on this wretched one - Be pleased with this unfortunate soul.
PUNDIT II	: Ah, this infidel is a great devotee! He knows the holy scriptures.
PUNDIT I	: (*sneering*) Come, let's go. We have not earned a little since morning as we have seen this infidel's face. It is not auspicious for us until he is driven out of here. Guards! Can't you see? An infidel has been hanging out here for a month tarnishing the Lion Gate? How are you guarding the door?
GUARD I	: How can we, the ignorant folk, drive him out when, the great pundits are keeping quiet. Moreover, we hear that he has submitted his application to the Committee of Pundits.
PUNDIT I	: His prayer has been rejected. You can now drive him out.

PUNDIT II	: Drive him out now. (*sneering*) This shameless fellow is very cunning. He wants to get the decision without spending a pie.
KALAPAHAD:	Oh, my Lord! This sinner has come with a great hope. - Please don't disappoint me. Please infuse some good will in your servitors. Redeem the sinners!
GUARD I	: Eh, hypocrite, get up and give way.
PUNDIT II	: Eh, is he a pilgrim that you beg of him? Beat this shameless fellow. - Give him a good beating.
GUARDS	: Hit him. Hit him hard! (*Beating Kalapahad.*)
KALAPAHAD:	Oh, my Lord! Did You order punishment for me? How, being merciful, did you consider it my punishment? Well, this sinner will gladly enjoy your punishment. - This criminal will accept this punishment gladly. If this is Your command for my atonement, this sinner will certainly be redeemed of his sins. This outcaste can again enter into the Hindu society.
PUNDIT I	: Arey, is this shameless fellow pretending to be asleep? - He sleeping like a dead body. Eh, drag him out. (*While beating Kalapahad, Dulia enters.*)
DULIA	: Oh, Lord of my life! What a scene! How horrible! (*embraces Kalapahad.*)
PUNDIT II	: Arey, this shameless fellow has a woman with him. – Beat him. - Beat him well. Beat this shameless woman too. (*While beating, Dulia collapses and Firoja enters.*)

FIROJA	: Oh, the meanest of mankind! Demons! What are you doing?
PUNDIT II	: Here is another. Beat her. (*Beats her.*) (*Golap enters.*)
GOLAP	: What a heinous act! - What a torture it is before the Lord of the Universe! - Tormenting a woman! Inflicting pain on a devotee of the Lord! Unbearable! It's simply intolerable! Oh, servitors - oh, Pundits, is it the evidence of your knowledge of the scriptures? Is it the example of your righteousness? Is this how you are contributing to the glory of Hinduism? Is this how you are singing the glory of Lord Jagannath? Fie on you! How ignorant the Pundits these days are! How mean the servitors these days are! Oh, Aryans ... oh, unholy men, stop beating. Repent for your misdeeds. Beg apology.
PUNDIT II	: Good heavens! This boy is very smart. Beat him; he is one of them. (*beats Golap*)
GOLAP	: Oh, Lord of the Universe! What a filthy show this is!
PUNDIT I	: Arey, this infidel is awake. (*attempts to beat Kalapahad.*)
GOLAP	: Beat me. - Beat me as much as you can. I can't see this torture on him. I can't tolerate such a downfall of Hinduism. (*Golap attempts to obstruct the servitors. They beat him and he falls down.*)
KALAPAHAD:	(*gets up furiously.*) Is this the conduct of a Hindu? Is it Hinduism? How mean souls you are! I can't tolerate it any more. I could

	tolerate as long as you were torturing me. I also tolerated the torture on my kinsfolk. - And now you are inflicting pain on our protector. Intolerable! - Intolerable!
PUNDIT II	: Arey, this shameless fellow is getting angry. Come, let's go way. (*attempting to flee.*)
KALAPAHAD:	Don't flee, rats. You needn't fear. I don't want to debase my hands by beating you. It is also not right atonement for your sins. Do you want to hear what amends I have planned for you? Will you like to hear what I have planned for your religion? Do you want to hear what penalty I have imagined for your deities? Halt. - Enlarge your ears. - Fix your gaze. - Check the beatings of your heart.
All	: (*in surprise*) What? What do you say?
GOLAP	: Please be calm, my lord.
KALAPAHAD:	Listen to me, devils. The treatment you meted out to this innocent girl, the cruelty you inflicted on this tender boy; the conduct, the torture, the misery that I have suffered, the distress that I have had in my nerves, will be adequately recompensed. I'll give similar treatment to very Hindu girl, boy, and old man.
GOLAP	: Please be calm, my lord. - Be calm -
KALAPAHAD:	It is not all, devils. I shall smash into smithereens the lifeless, motionless, wood idol of the presiding deity of the religion that imparts such evil knowledge and has declined into such nefarious state. I

shall very soon pull down this glorious temple of immortal fame, the pride of this race and the venerated destination of all pilgrims. I shall submerge this holy Puri Dham in the sea that symbolises oblivion. At that time, the whole kingdom turning pale as a corpse, the whole Bharatvarsha shaking like a volcanic eruption, the whole earth batting an eye will witness that the Bay of Bengal is sanguine with the flow of blood. - The earth has been buried deep in the clasp of the dead bodies. - The wind has been still with the souls of the dead bodies. - All of you will clamour in one voice. – The earth and the sky will echo the answer that the Hindu has lost its race - lost its religion – lost its deity and its glorious temple.

GOLAP : My lord! Oh, my lord!
(*All look aghast.*)
(*Curtain*)

ACT III
SCENE I
The Council Chamber of Akbar.

AKBAR : What treachery! What a traitor!
BIRBAL : You can see for yourself, Badshah. You didn't believe in me, did you?
AKBAR : Oh, Jester! Administration is not possible without trust.
BIRBAL : But for the jester it is reversed.
AKBAR : How is it? Do I not trust you? You are my chief courtier.

BIRBAL : Chief Courtier, indeed! But as long as I am in this attire and in this court. You certainly believe in me but as long as I converse with you alone, but not when you listen to others' discourse.

AKBAR : (*laughing.*) Your wise words are so meaningful that it is impossible for me to understand them.

BIRBAL : It will be really so. The words of the poor are bare. Had they been decorative, they would have been fit for the Badshah to listen to them.

AKBAR : (*smiling.*) Well, what's the matter?

BIRBAL : Remember Katalu.

AKBAR : Is it a current matter?

BIRBAL : No, no, a thing of the past. It was during your journey for cajoling. You laughed at this jester's words.

AKBAR : (*laughing.*) The wise words of the jester are not easy to understand. (*gravely.*) Birbal, is it that Katalu whom I have adored as a son since his childhood? Is he the same person whom I have given shelter and promoted him from a mere soldier to a General? It never occurred to me - I have never dreamt that the same Katalu will be such an ungrateful wretch - such a heinous traitor. But, Birbal, I have never come across such attitude in him before.

BIRBAL : How can you see it, Your Majesty? His heart was not possessed with the Goddess of jealousy then.
(*Mukunda Deb enters.*)

MUKUNDA : Greetings, Badshah!
AKBAR : Greetings, Oh King! But why did you address me as 'Badshah' instead of 'friend'?
MUKUNDA : Can this pauper be ever worthy of friendship of Badshah?
AKBAR : A pauper? You are a pauper before Lord Jagannath. You are the greatest warrior. You are a sovereign ruler; a genuine friend.
MUKUNDA : I beg your forgiveness, friend. You are needlessly praising me. It pains me.
AKBAR : It is also painful for me that I am unable to praise a warrior appropriately - sing in praise of a wise person. Tell me, dear friend, 'which friend can selflessly help an infidel friend to such an extent without caring for his own life only for the sake of a treaty?'
MUKUNDA : Badshah! -
AKBAR : Again -
MUKUNDA : But, I could not help you, friend.
AKBAR : Why not? – it's true that you could not win the war because of the treachery of Katalu and Rahamat Khan and because of your small army. But have you given up your best efforts? It is, of course, for that purpose you have come to me.
MUKUNDA : Leave it, dear friend. Let me, please, take your leave today. I won't rest in peace until I win the war and send the traitors to you.
AKBAR : No, dear friend, I won't leave you today. Have complete rest for some days here until you regain your strength.
(*Mansingh enters.*)

MANSINGH	:	Emperor, only ten thousand soldiers have been collected.
MUKUNDA	:	It's enough. I have sent for more soldiers from my kingdom.
MANSINGH	:	(*aside, with a heavy sigh*) My kingdom! My own soldiers! What can be a prouder thing for a king? What can be a more fortunate thing for a king?
MUKUNDA	:	Are they all ready, oh king?
MANSINGH	:	(*aside*) King! Who is the king? One who has lost his freedom? This hanger-on! Fie on me! To address this damn Kshatriya as 'king' is a dishonour to the position of the king. Demeaning kingship! (*openly*) They are all ready, oh king.
MUKUNDA	:	Dear friend, I need not waste time in vain when everybody is ready.
AKBAR	:	Dear friend, shouldn't you keep the request of a friend?
MUKUNDA	:	Dear friend, let me first finish the friend's work. Then, I have no objection to enjoy leisure as long as you wish.
AKBAR	:	Dear friend, you are indeed my good friend. Come, let's enjoy our friendship.
MUKUNDA	:	How fortunate this humble man is! I have the good fortune to have the friendly embrace of the emperor of Hindustan.
AKBAR	:	This humble man is also fortunate enough to have the friendly embrace of the crown jewel of the Hindus. Come, dear friend, to my parlour.
MUKUNDA	:	Please come, dear friend, dear jester. (*Akbar and Mukunda Deb exit.*)

MANSINGH	: (*aside*) Mukunda Deb is a Kshatriya. Mansingh is a Kshatriya too. One is a friend and the other is a slave. One is on the throne and the other is at the feet. The difference is between the earth and the sky, between heaven and hell.
BIRBAL	: Don't be sad, friend. Come, let's embrace each other. When masters embrace each other, why not the servants?
GUARD	: Oh king! Oh Punditji! Badshah is waiting for you.
MANSINGH	: Is he waiting for us or commanding us to come? (*aside*) What a shame! What a shame! Is the valour of a Kshatriya as well as his prowess meant for slavery?
BIRBAL	: Let's go, dear. Command is issued. (*to guard*) Dear friend, please lead us. Why do you hesitate? You are a servant. – I am a servant too. You guard Badshah's door. – We guard his moods. – This is the only difference. Let's go, friend. (*Birbal rests his arm on the guard's shoulder and both of them exit.*)
MANSINGH	: You are right, jester. (*Exit.*) (*Curtain*)

SCENE II
Entertainment Hall.
(Rahamat and Abdullah are present)

RAHAMAT	: Eh boy, what's your name?
ABDULLAH	: My name – my name is 'Boy'.
RAHAMAT	: Stupid boy. I ask you your name.

ABDULLAH	:	You are repeatedly addressing me as 'Boy'. Then call me by that name.
RAHAMAT	:	OK, then. You are a good boy. Your name is Jalil.
ABDULLAH	:	Yes, Your Honour. My name is Jalil.
RAHAMAT	:	Who am I?
ABDULLAH	:	You are the Nawab.
KATALU	:	Who am I?
ABDULLAH	:	You are the Badshah.
RAHAMAT	:	No, I am Badshah.
KATALU	:	No, I am Badshah.
RAHAMAT	:	Jalil, tell me correctly, who I am.
KATALU	:	Jalil, speak the truth. Who am I?
ABDULLAH	:	Please wait a little. I'll make you understand the truth. You have killed the Nawab. Therefore, you are the Nawab. You have made him the Nawab by cheating on the Badshah. Therefore, you are the Badshah.
KATALU & RAHAMAT	:	(*patting Abdullah's back.*) You are right. You are right. You are a good boy. (*looking at a distance*) Where do these dancers come from? Who has called for them?
ABDULLAH	:	I have.
KATALU & RAHAMAT	:	You are a good boy. Get wine for us. Sing, women. - Sing a sweet song. Let's have some fun.

(*Dancers sing.*)

(Song)
Play the harp, ready the dancers
Let the night sway in a playful mood
Sing to a tune sweet as nectar,

Tinged with romance, thrill and love.
Dance to the tune of cuckoo's song,
With rhythmic tunes of anklets
Like Cupid and his consort, decked in flowers,
Sing and dance with numerous poses.

      (*Abdullah is pouring wine into the decanters while the singers and dancers are performing, and Rahamat and Katalu were drinking. Gradually both of them fall asleep.*)

ABDULLAH : (*gives up his disguise*) Go away dancers. Your work is over.

DANCERS : As you wish, prince. (*Exit.*)

ABDULLAH : Let me finish my job now. (*brings out a knife*) This is the knife you have given me, Rahamat. I attempted to kill brother-like Kalapahad with this knife and tried to ruin sister Dulia. Allah saved me. What have I done now? I have stained the blade of this knife with the holy blood of my uncle. I have drunk the blood of a human being, a king and a father as well. Ha! Ha! Ha! Ha! I am the true son of a father, true subject of a kingdom. Now, see how I am going to a be good friend to the friend whose advice made me so.

(*While he was going to stab Rahamat there is a gunshot from the background and Abdul collapses. Kalapahad enters. Rahamat and Katalu get up.*)

KALAPAHAD: Get up immediately, Nawab Saheb. Who is it? Where is the Nawab? This is Rahamat Ali.

ABDULLAH : Oh, I could not pay back the traitor in

	his own coins. I couldn't fulfil my desire. Uncle! Uncle!
KALAPAHAD:	Who is here? Is this Abdul?
ABDULLAH :	Whose voice is this?
KALAPAHAD:	Abdul!
ABDULLAH :	Kalapahad! Brother, have you really come back?
KALAPAHAD:	Oh, what did I do, brother?
ABDULLAH :	You have not done anything wrong. My sin has recoiled on me.
KALAPAHAD:	Which sin have you paid for, brother?
ABDULLAH :	Which sin? Is my retribution complete? My sin will be recompensed with my life.
KALAPAHAD:	Which sin, brother?
ABDULLAH :	Which sin? To speak about the sin is a sin. To hear about the sin is a sin.
KALAPAHAD:	Don't add to my eagerness, brother. Tell me which sin have you committed?
ABDULLAH :	Uh, what a sin! It is homicide, regicide and patricide at the same time.
KALAPAHAD:	What do you say, Abdul? Is Nawab Saheb no more? Is father no more?
ABDULLAH :	He is here. Look at the heavens. Mark him among the stars. How he is sitting in a celestial seat, clad in celestial raiment with a heavenly hallow. How he raises his eye brows at me! How he bites his lips!
KALAPAHAD:	Abdul! Abdul!
ABDULLAH :	Now I understand, brother. Give me a knife, brother. This traitor has not been punished. This sinner is not yet punished. (*falls down while trying to get up*) I could not discharge my duties.

KALAPAHAD: Which duty, brother?
ABDULLAH : To punish the traitor – the sinful Rahamat.
KALAPAHAD: I do understand everything, brother. This worst sinner Rahamat is the cause of all devastation. Is there anybody here?
(*A soldier enters.*)
SOLDIER : Yes, Your Highness.
KALAPAHAD: Put him in chains. (*looking at Katalu*) Who are you?
KATALU : I am Ka… Ka…
KALAPAHAD: Speak up immediately. Who are you?
KATALU : Your Majesty, I am Katalu.
SOLDIER : Your Majesty. He is the Mughal commander, Katalu. He has treacherously joined us. He is a good friend of our commander.
KALAPAHAD: He too is a traitor. Unite both the friends. (*Katalu is put in chains.*) Alas, I could not see the Nawab. Abdul! Brother, what did I do? (*embraces Abdul*)
ABDULLAH : Don't be sorry, brother. Let me depart in peace. Where is Dulia, brother? She is my own sister. Alas, how unfairly I have treated her! She has cared for me as her brother but I was so sinful that I tortured her. What a sin I have committed! Should I ever be forgiven?
(*Dulia enters.*)
DULIA : Of course, you should be. – Who is this dying person?
KALAPAHAD: (*getting up*) Dulia, I have committed a grave sin. I have wrought a great ruin.
DULIA : What sin! What ruin, Oh, Lord of my Life!

ABDULLAH	:	Nothing, my sister.
DULIA	:	Who? Brother? (*goes near him*)
ABDULLAH	:	No, sister. I am your enemy. How can a demon like me take pride in a goddess-like sister as you?
DULIA	:	Brother Abdul, why are you in such a misery? (*embraces Abdul*)
ABDULLAH	:	This is my good luck, sister. Come sister, my dear sister, I have never cared for you as long as I lived. Let me make my life meaningful at the time of this final journey by putting a kiss on you.
DULIA	:	Brother, why are you taking back the nectar you have given to me? Are you really leaving your dear sister alone? Why are you depriving me of your brotherly love?
KALAPAHAD:		Oh, the Lord of my heart! I have brought this ruin on you.
DULIA	:	How so?
KALAPAHAD:		I have shot Abdul with my own pistol.
DULIA	:	With your pistol?
ABDULLAH	:	Sister, it is the design of the Heavens. It is the retribution of my sin. The real killer of me is – the one in whose instigation I have committed the sin of killing my father.
DULIA	:	What are you telling, brother?
ABDULLAH	:	This demon – this sinner, Dulia. My duties – your search – restoring the kingship is complete. The rest – revenge for the murder of our father and your brother - punishment for this wretched Rahamat.
KALAPAHAD:		I accept that responsibility, brother.

ABDULLAH	:	I am now assured. Forgive me, sister. Give me shelter in your lap. Dul... (*dies.*)
DULIA	:	Alas, father is no more. Now, father-like brother is no more. I am now deprived of the love of my father and brother.
KALAPAHAD	:	Oh, the Lord of my heart! Don't worry. We can get peace of heart when these demons shed their last drop of blood.
GOLAP	:	Your Majesty, how are you going to cool your soul with bloodshed? Allah, the Almighty, does not intend bloodshed as a means of atonement.
KALAPAHAD	:	This small bloodshed is not Allah's will. It is only a small fraction of the greater bloodshed I have in mind.
GOLAP	:	My Lord. Give up your oath. Please desist from such cruel thoughts. How can you, being a human, act like a demon? How can you, being rational, be a beast? What shall the gods in Heaven say? What shall the Nagas under the earth say? What shall the beings on earth say?
KALAPAHAD	:	Ha! Ha! Shall I abandon my promises fearing scandals? Even if Vasuki with his one thousand tongues speaks ill of me, even if lord Brahma with his four mouths heaps indignation on me, even if all the animal world tarnishes my honour, my promises shall remain constant.
GOLAP	:	You may ignore dishonour, My Lord, but how can you ignore regard for righteousness? Please introspect, and pay heed to the cries of mercy arising from

	your heart. - Have a feeling of compassion in your heart; your determination, and your resolute will shall disappear.
KALAPAHAD:	Shut up, boy. Oh, my heart, why are you wavering? Be as firm as Mountain Mandar. Why are beastly instincts in me sedate? Burn with radiance like the sacrificial fire, and burn all my tender instincts to cinders. May all my worldly ties be blown into smithereens. Let my breath be filled with the force of a gale. Let the sea roar like thunder. Let me be a killer of humans, be an ogre, and greedy of human blood. I must carry out my oath. I'll abolish the Hindu religion so that there shall be none of it on earth. I'll ruin the Hindu state and relegate it into hell. I'll so destroy the Hindu race that there shall be all races but the Hindus.
KATALU :	Your Lordship, if the life of this meanest of mankind is spared, this slave will render immense help to you in your noble mission.
RAHAMAT :	I do have the same wish, My Lord.
KALAPAHAD:	(*aside*) Such help is necessary. I need the help of a traitor, an assassin to achieve my goal. (*to the audience*) Katalu, I grant you your life and you shall hence be my Chief Commander.
KATALU :	Yah Allah! As you wish, My Lord. (*Greets*)
RAHAMAT :	Please, spare my life, My Lord.
KALAPAHAD:	Well, I assure you your life too.
DULIA :	But I won't spare their life, My Lord. A

	slaughterer begging for life before justice! – Sparing the life of the assassin of a father before his daughter! – Sparing the life of the murderer of a brother before his sister! – Impossible! – Certainly impossible!
KALAPAHAD:	Well, you can dispense justice for Rahamat.
DULIA :	Shall I dispense justice? What justice shall I advance? Which punishment will be fit for him? How can I decide? My Lord, please dispense justice for Rahamat.
KALAPAHAD:	No, darling! You have to punish the murderer of your father and brother with death sentence. Take this prisoner away and throw him into the dark cell till he is executed. Accompany with him, Katalu.
RAHAMAT :	Dear Princess!

(*Katalu and soldiers exit with the prisoner.*)

DULIA :	Alas, brother! Why did you leave your sister behind? (*clasps Abdul.*)
KALAPAHAD:	There is no time for shedding tears now, darling. It's time for revenge – revenge. (*Kalapahad hurriedly exits.*)
GOLAP :	Sister! Sister! Oh Lord, is this your design? (*Exit.*)

(*Curtain*)

SCENE III
Gynaecium.

GOLAP :	Alas, I couldn't anyhow make him understand. Let me try if I can do anything through Dulia. Of course, I could somewhat pacify Dulia. – Head for a head! – Revenge for a kin's murder with

the murder of the murderer! – Impossible. Our peace of mind lies in meditation on the God Almighty, the giver of peace. The right revenge comprises in doing good to the preparator of the evil.

(Song)

Be kind to me, Oh Lord of all orphans,
Put an end to my misery.
May the grey desert of my heart
Be green with vegetation.
How I have planted the seeds of desire
To offer flowers and fruits at your feet
As they grow into trees to blossom
Now an enemy has uprooted each plant,
Leaving me as an orphan.

(*Kalapahad enters.*)

KALAPAHAD: What memory wakes up in you? What image is reflected in your mind, Golap?

GOLAP : Your Majesty!

KALAPAHAD: Who are you? Speak the truth.

GOLAP : This humble slave has revealed my identity several times to you, Your Majesty.

KALAPAHAD: But I don't believe in them. You come of Bengal – a Hindu by religion – a conservative Brahmin. – Still you are serving a Muslim. – It's surprising!

GOLAP : What is there to be surprised about, Your Majesty? A Hindu cannot become a Muslim by serving a Muslim. One's caste cannot be affected by serving an infidel. An individual's race, religious beliefs, conduct, bearings and attitude to life completely depend on him. Particularly,

		I am a slave to love. I serve those who care for me.
KALAPAHAD:		How could you learn these noble things, Golap?
GOLAP	:	I don't know it, Your Majesty. However, it is my faith; my conviction, Your Majesty.
KALAPAHAD:		Are you being looked after well here?
GOLAP	:	Very much.
KALAPAHAD:		How could you know it?
GOLAP	:	That you are talking to me sweetly being a master – from this.
KALAPAHAD:		Well, you should love me in return.
GOLAP	:	I very much should. I should worship you.
KALAPAHAD:		Will you carry out what I say?
GOLAP	:	I'll consider.
KALAPAHAD:		Then you are not a true servant.
GOLAP	:	Then, relieve me of your service.
KALAPAHAD:		Relieve you! Impossible!
GOLAP	:	This is how you admit that I am a suitable servant. It is an evidence of profound affection you have for me.
KALAPAHAD:		True, Golap. The sweetness in your tender rosy face, and the fascinating sweetness in your rosy words contain such sweetness, such enchantment that my heart and soul are sold to you –absorbed in you.
GOLAP	:	It is very kind of you, Your Majesty.
KALAPAHAD:		You should not think that I am revealing my false love and affection to you as a way of my gratitude for you because you have suffered unbearable woes at that unholy place of the Hindus and for the sacrifice you have done for me. My stony heart is

	moved with uncanny love as soon as I see you. All the while I feel that all my peace lies in you – all my happiness lies in you. Dear Golap, I have never felt so much of love and affection for anybody. Well, you have been with us for a pretty long time but you have never asked for any compensation for it. You have never raised that issue anywhere even in conversation Don't you have any dependants on you?
GOLAP	: I have everybody, Your Majesty. By the grace of God, I have never been in want.
KALAPAHAD:	Well, you are an amateur attender. That's why you please me so much. But I should reward you for your work
GOLAP	: You need not worry about that now, Your Majesty. I shall beg of you when I feel the need.
KALAPAHAD:	Well, be it so.
	(*The eunuch enters.*)
EUNUCH	: Your Majesty, the messenger has arrived. There is some serious work to attend.
	(*DULIA: enters.*)
DULIA	: What kind of serious work?
KALAPAHAD:	I am coming soon, darling.
	(*Kalapahad and the eunuch exit.*)
GOLAP	: Begum Sahiba!
DULIA	: Why the same old address?
GOLAP	: Sorry, sister. Do you remember what I have said?
DULIA	: Yes, brother. I'm trying to remember as far as possible.
GOLAP	: Your Majesty –

DULIA	:	Why again such address?
GOLAP	:	I often forget, sister. Well, you know sister that anything good or bad about a religion does not depend on the activities of a few greedy, selfish followers of that religion.
DULIA	:	I know it very well, brother. I have also learnt from you what I did not know earlier. Listen to me brother, though I am a Muslim, I have profound knowledge of Hinduism. Though my husband is against Hinduism, I have still complete faith in it. Though Hindus and Muslims are known as Kafirs and Yavanas respectively, I make no difference between these two religions.
GOLAP	:	I wish he had such feelings and beliefs in him.
DULIA	:	You needn't worry, brother. If Allah wills everything is possible. Lord Jagannath's will shall prevail.
GOLAP	:	We should also have sincere efforts in this regard.
DULIA	:	That's right. But brother, aren't the people of his faith responsible for my husband's madness for ruining his own creed? Aren't they at fault?
GOLAP	:	Or course, they are responsible – Of course, they are at fault. However, it is the responsibility of humans to remove all dirt and dung from their own religion.
DULIA	:	It's their primary duty. I too remember my duty, brother – revenge – avenging the murder of my father and brother.
GOLAP	:	Why this infernal thought, sister? Blood for

blood again? Does revenge for bloodshed lie in bloodshed? You shall commit sin by the bloodshed that leads to sin! You shall double the unrest by bloodshed that leads to unrest! To think of such revenge is sheer beastly, sheer abnormality. Such a desire for peace is illusion – a delusion.

DULIA : How can I, being a bereaved daughter as well as sister, calmly watch the slaughterer of my father and brother peacefully enjoying his days?

GOLAP : Sister, a sinner can never be at ease. He can only be at rest in death. Moreover, it's not our duty to bother about the crime committed nor the punishment for the sinner. We should leave the responsibility of dispensing justice to Him who is the Judge of virtue and vice, the Executer of punishment or reward and be rest assured. We should have staunch faith in Him. He is the only redeemer who will save us from our sorrow. He can only bless us with peace and fill our anguished soul with peace.

DULIA : Who are you, brother, appearing like the sun in this dark firmament – like a sea in this dreary desert?

GOLAP : I am only your ever-loyal brother.

DULIA : Allah! You are indeed the redeemer of suffering. You are indeed the giver of peace.

(*Kalapahad enters.*)

KALAPAHAD: It's a very good piece of news, Dulia.

DULIA	:	What good news, O Lord of my Heart?
KALAPAHAD:		Mukunda Dev has attacked Bengal.
DULIA	:	What is the good news then?
KALAPAHAD:		Isn't it a piece of good news? Mukunda Dev is the crowning jewel of the Hindus – emperor of the Hindus. If I can defeat this glorious Hindu emperor, if I can execute him under the sword of an executor, the anguish of my revenge can be pacified a little.
DULIA	:	O Lord of my Heart! Give up this devilish oath. As a wise person, you should not lose your sense of duty.
GOLAP	:	As a religious person, you should not stray from religion.
KALAPAHAD:		Ha! Ha! Ha! Ha! You are a Hindu, Golap. That's why it is your idea of religion.
GOLAP	:	Your Highness, had I been that partial, I would not, as a Hindu, have served an enemy of the Hindus.
KALAPAHAD:		(*looks at him with surprise.*)
GOLAP	:	Please tell, your Highness, you have sworn that you will ruin all Hindus even if he is an infant or, boy or an old man. Why are you so kind enough to spare me?
KALAPAHAD:		Why?
DULIA	:	O Lord of my Life! I touch your feet and pray you to give up this devilish oath.
GOLAP	:	This humble servant of yours, too, have this prayer, your Highness.
KALAPAHAD:		(*Aside*) No. No, my heart! Don't be soft. (*Aloud*) Dulia, you belong to the Gynaecium. Golap, you are a slave. Both of

you rightfully belong to the inner palace. Confine yourself to home. You don't have the right to enter into this intricate matter. Let me go. I have to prepare myself soon. (*Kalapahad exits.*)
(*Dulia feels upset while looking at disappearing Kalapahad.*)

GOLAP : Give up vain worries, sister. Think for once. – How flimsy is a woman in the eyes of men! How trivial the duty of a wife is!

DULIA : Brother!

GOLAP : Come, sister. However insignificant a man does think of his woman, however inconsequential he may consider her, a wife must do her rightful duty. You should mind the duty of a wife.

DULIA : Please, tell brother, what should I do?

GOLAP : What appropriate duty? To save your husband from committing sin – to check him from straying from his righteous path.

DULIA : Brother, my husband is my Lord. Even if he is a sinner, he is my Lord. How can I go against his will?

GOLAP : Sister, aren't you neglecting the duties as a wife?

DULIA : How, brother? The duty of a wife is to love her husband wholeheartedly. Have I not done it so?

GOLAP : How have you done it? Is it the real love? Would he follow the path of sin so quickly, if you really loved him? If you had the right sense of duty, your husband would not be so enthusiastic to follow the wrong path. Sister, the right sense of duty propels a wife to urge her husband to follow the right path even at the cost of her life. It is true love that inspires her to sacrifice her own peace and happiness to set up her husband in righteous peace and happiness.

DULIA : Golap! Golap! Who are you brother in disguise? You have opened my closed eyes. You have illumined my hard heart. Come brother teach me the duties of a consort.

GOLAP : Come sister. Teach this slave the duties proper for him. Come. (*Both exit.*)

(*Curtain*)

SCENE IV
A Camp in the Battlefield.

(*Mukunda Dev is worried.*)

MUKUNDA : Why didn't my platoon of soldiers from Utkal reach yet? I cannot be at rest until they arrive. Every moment I apprehend Kalapahad's attack on us. (*Painful screaming of Mukunda Dev's soldiers is heard from the background.*) What is it? Why this screaming? O Lord Jagannath, pray help us. (*about to leave*)

(*Kalapahad enters.*)

KALAPAHAD: Help, Lord Jagannath! O Mukunda Dev, crowning glory of the Hindus. You shall be imprisoned by a Yavana. I shall offer my oblation with your blood tomorrow and douse the fire of my revenge a little.

MUKUNDA : Who are you? Are you a human or a monster?

KALAPAHAD: I'm a monster. Can't you recognise Monster Kalapahad?

MUKUNDA : O Kalapahad!

KALAPAHAD: Ha! Ha! Ha! Can't you recognise Kalapahad? Being a Hindu can't you recognise Kalapahad? Ha! Ha! Ha!

MUKUNDA : What unearthly countenance have you put up, Commander?

KALAPAHAD: Did I have this hellish countenance of my own accord or your Hindu brothers have compelled me to have this?

MUKUNDA : I can't follow you, Commander.

KALAPAHAD: You needn't understand. I want blood – the Hindu blood – only the Hindu blood

MUKUNDA : What fierce figure! Brows are raised as if in fiendish loathing! Eyes are red as if due to diabolic anger! The whole body is shuddering in a strange shiver! Commander, you are a warrior. Be calm.

KALAPAHAD: I shall be calm only after I drink your blood, Mukunda, after I bring ruin to Hindu religion, after I uproot Hinduism.

MUKUNDA : Are you an infidel or a Chandal?

KALAPAHAD: I'm a Chandal. I am a Chandal for the race I was born in. I am a Chandal for the land where I was first consecrated.

MUKUNDA : (*Aside.*) What a Chandal! Can a person be such a devil when he deserts his religion?

KALAPHAD : Hurry up, Mukunda Dev, surrender yourself immediately. I cannot put up with my thirst for Hindu blood any longer.

MUKUNDA : Ha! Ha! Ha! Do you think that I'm a weak child, or a timid dastard?
KALAPAHAD: You are gallant, brave and a valiant youth too. But –
MUKUNDA : But what?
KALAPAHAD: Helpless.
MUKUNDA : Is Mukunda Dev helpless!
KALAPHAD. I only know it.
MUKUNDA : Do you know, Commander, with the help of a sword Mukunda Dev alone can bravely encounter thousands of soldiers?
KALAPAHAD: (*smiling*) If you can you get such help –
MUKUNDA : Is anybody here?
(*Katalu and Mughals enter.*)
KATALU : At your service, please.
MUKUNDA : This is Katalu. Are these Mughals?
(*Background voice: "O Emperor! – Flee. – Flee. – Treachery. – Treachery."*)
What do I hear? It's the pitiable cry of the soldiers of Utkal.
(*Background voice : "O I'm dying" – "I'm dying".*)
It's the pitiable cry of the dying. Be not afraid, soldiers.
(*Mukunda Dev is about to leave.*)
KATALU : (*drawing his sword*) Tarry, O Mukunda Dev.
KALAPAHAD: Ha! Ha! Ha! Mukunda Dev, where is your sword? Where are your soldiers from Utkal? Under whose control are your Mughal soldiers? Vain airs! Vain confidence! Katalu, do your job.
(*Katalu attempts to imprison Mukunda Dev.*)

MUKUNDA   : Beware, how dare you, being a jackal, touch the body of a lion?

KALAPAHAD: Great shame, Mukunda Dev, Great shame. It's high time that a lion was being imprisoned by a jackal.

MUKUNDA   : (*aside*) I am out of my mind; I forget that a helpless lion is sometimes kicked by a jackal.

KALAPAHAD: Katalu, why do you wait? Do your job.

KATALU   : (*approaching Mukunda Dev timidly puts chains on him.*) Now, tell everybody, who is the lion and who's the jackal?

MUKUNDA   : (*aside*) What is predestined cannot be overcome.

KALAPAHAD: Guide the prisoner to the prison. It's my order that none but me can visit him or talk to him.

KATALU   : Yes, Your Majesty. Let's go, O King.

MUKUNDA   : Before I go, let me tell you Mughals, is it your devotion for the king? Is this your humanity? – You have eaten your king's food – have been brought up under his protection. Still, how do you raise arms against him? – Why are you so eager to ruin your protector?

(*Silence prevails among the MUGHALS*)

KALAPAHAD: Hurry up.

MUKUNDA   : (*while leaving*) What kind of character do you show today, O warriors? What kind of meanness is this, O Mughals? If at all you are true Mughals, true followers of holy Islam, real warriors, then give up your meanness. – Give up treachery. – Raise your arms with heroic spirit

	in support of your father-like king. – Sacrifice your life for your benefactor as a tree does.
MUGHALS	: O Emperor! O Emperor!
KALAPAHAD:	Hurry up, Commander, take him away immediately.

(*Katalu drags Mukunda Dev away.*)

KALAPAHAD: O Mughals, are you infidels? Are you mean Kafirs? You believe in the words of a Kafir, – get excited by his words. Do you know, brothers, what the intention of this mean Kafir is? – To subjugate the followers of holy Islam. – To convert holy Islam into his unholy kafir religion.

MUGHALS : How dare he?

KALAPAHAD: Listen brothers, I have no enmity with your Badshah Akbar. – Enmity with him has disappeared with the death of Nawab Suleman. Badshah Akbar is my Badshah too. The glory be to Badshah Akbar!

MUGHALS : The glory be to Badshah Akbar!

KALAPAHAD: Come brothers, we shall join hands and scream "Allah Ho Akbar" so loudly as to pierce the earth and the sky and take an oath to destroy the religion of the Kafirs, and make efforts to obliterate the names of the Kafirs.

MUGHALS : What are your commands for us, Nawab? We are all ready.

KALAPAHAD: Now, relax and enjoy yourselves. Come female singers and the party. (*Exit.*)

(*Mughals exit while enjoying the song and dance of the female singers. Kalapahad again enters from his secret place and looks at the Mughals with joy.)*

KALAPAHAD: Now, the King of the Hindus is really in prison. The king of the Hindu religion is really under my complete control. It is going to be Hindu's bloodshed tomorrow – the beginning of the fulfilment of my oath. Let me now take a little rest.
(Golap enters.)

GOLAP : Can you have rest, Your Highness?

KALAPAHAD: Why can't I? Who can't feel fresh and relaxed if a servant like Golap is in attendance?

GOLAP : But – can you reduce the pains and exhaustion of the heart?

KALAPAHAD: All worries disappear when I look at the rosy countenance of Golap and listen to her rosy words. – All my sorrows disappear.

GOLAP : But, if Golap (the rose) is in full bloom, it will look beautiful and spread its fragrance.

KALAPAHAD: My Golap (the rose) is ever in bloom. Oh, I see, why do you look so pale today, Golap?

GOLAP : An insect is biting, Your Highness.

KALAPAHAD: Insect? Which insect? Where is it?

GOLAP : You are the creator, Your Highness. Why do you ask me?

KALAPAHAD: Me? Give up riddles, Golap.

GOLAP : Well, please tell, Your Highness, who have you thrown into the dark prison today? Who are you going to kill by the executor tomorrow? By eliminating whose sacred name are you eager to hear the wailings of the Hindus?

KALAPAHAD: (*smiling*) It's Mukunda Deva's, the monarch of the Hindus who is imprisoned by me.

GOLAP : 'Of the prisoner Mukunda Deva', the Hindu King! How could you utter these words so easily? Didn't your tongue shrink? How could you so easily draw the image of death of the pious king, who is like the soul of the Hindus? Didn't your body shiver? How could you so easily tolerate the heaven-piercing wailing of the Hindus? Didn't your heart quiver? – O, Your Majesty!

KALAPAHAD: Golap, haven't you given up Hindu sentiments although you are staying with the Muslims?

GOLAP : Your Majesty, can the sun stop emitting heat even though it is enveloped by the clouds? Can the moon part with its coolness even though it is swallowed by Rahu?

KALAPAHAD: Then, it's now time for you to be sad, O boy. The Hindu monarch has been imprisoned. – Shed tears for him now. The holy king will be beheaded. – Pass out. The term 'Hindu' will, before long, be eliminated from the surface of the earth.

GOLAP : Your Majesty!

KALAPAHAD: I am helpless, boy. I'll destroy the Hindu empire. – Bring Hindu race to ruin. – Destroy the Hindu religion. – It is my oath. – It is my duty.

GOLAP : Then, allow me to do my duty, Your Highness.

KALAPAHAD: Your duty!

GOLAP : Do I not have any duty? Being a Hindu, do I not have any duty towards the Hindus? Can I, being a Hindu, be a silent witness when an enemy of the Hindus is going to ruin Hinduism? Can I be at peace when an antagonist of Hindu race is going to obliterate it? It's impossible!

KALAPAHAD: Ha! Ha! Ha! O boy, I see, you have not overcome your childishness. However, I am very glad to see your staunch faith in your religion.

GOLAP : (*Aside*) What a blunder I have done! I revealed my intention in the heat of excitement. (*Aloud*) Your Highness, please forgive me for my insolence.

KALAPAHAD: No, Golap, your begging apology is your insolence.

GOLAP : My Lord!

KALAPAHAD: What do you want to say?

GOLAP : (*being distraught*)

KALAPAHAD: Speak out, Golap. You needn't fear.

GOLAP : (*restraining herself*) Your Highness, will the Hindu king be executed tomorrow? Will Hindu religion be ruined?

KALAPAHAD: Yes, indeed.

GOLAP : Before the death sentence, I want to have a face to face encounter with the unfortunate Hindu monarch.

KALAPAHAD: You can see him in the execution ground.

GOLAP : No, no, Your Highness. This luckless woman wishes to listen to a few sermons and key lessons on religion.

KALAPAHAD: I see that you are very religious minded. (*Aside*) I too had the same attitude one day. (*Aloud*) Superstition! All Superstition! Well, when do you want to meet him?

GOLAP : Tonight. In the prison. Alone.

KALAPAHAD: Impossible. – Quite impossible. A personal meeting with a prisoner – that too at night. It is against my principles and commands.

GOLAP : Your Majesty, please it's my humble request to grant my wish in lieu of the remuneration for my long service.

KALAPAHAD: Request! it's not a request. Your dues are too insignificant. – very insignificant. I am now giving you an insignia bearing my name.

GOLAP : Victory to Nawab Bahadur. (*Both exit.*)
(Curtain.)

SCENE V
A Room in the Prison.
(*Mukunda Dev is alone.*)

MUKUNDA : Go away, night. You are very fortunate. You have taken leave of me today without being tarnished. Come, Goddess Morning. Don't be shy. I know that your mind is clear. But, what can you do? Evil has now taken the upper hand. Injustice now rules. Why do you cry? Why are you shedding tears in vain? Do you feel that a convert can have compassion for the people of his original religion? Can a traitor's sword ever be blunted? Can the flow of my cold blood be checked? Impossible! Oh, Lord Jagannath! Shall I have to sacrifice my life like goats and sheep in chains without a fight? – Like a timid coward? Oh, how miserable for a Kshatriya! – What misery for a chivalrous warrior!

(*Golap enters with a sword in hand.*)

GOLAP	:	How painful it is for this poor soul!
MUKUNDA	:	(*with astonishment*) Who are you, O boy?
GOLAP	:	I'm an unfortunate Hindu, O pious King!
MUKUNDA	:	Do you belong to this Muslim family?
GOLAP	:	Yes, O holy King!
MUKUNDA	:	Why do you tell this prisoner that you are a Hindu? Are you mocking me?
GOLAP	:	I'm not mocking, O King, trust me.
MUKUNDA	:	How can I trust you? Sword in hand – appearing at night – meeting the prisoner alone – should I trust you? You have been sent to assassin me surreptitiously.
GOLAP	:	To rescue you secretly, O King.
MUKUNDA	:	To rescue me secretly! (*staring surprisingly*)
GOLAP	:	Have faith in this humble soul, O pious King.
MUKUNDA	:	What faith, O boy? – The faith that I had in my subordinates for which I am forced to undergo a poor miserable life? – Is it the same kind of faith? To have faith in you – a mere boy – a boy living in the enemy's house. – Impossible! – Impossible!
GOLAP	:	(*kneeling down and lowering the head*) My Lord! Trust this humble soul.
MUKUNDA	:	(*aside*) This is an innocent boy. (*aloud*)

	Well, get up boy. But, tell me who is this generous human who volunteers to save my life? Who is this kind soul who is so eager to save my life?
GOLAP	: It is He, O King, who is so eager. – It is He who offers His help. He is so generous that He looks after the high and the low without any discrimination. – Because of whose mercy the planets in the sky, flora and fauna on earth are engaged in bringing up the beings.
MUKUNDA	: I have now faith in you, O boy. You are not an ordinary boy. – You are an angel sent to rescue the sinner. *(looking upwards)* Oh Generous One! Oh Merciful! I bow at your lotus feet. *(bows his head.)* You too are venerated for me, O boy. *(bows his head.)*
GOLAP	: Please forgive this poor soul, O Holy King. This poor soul is only doing his duty.
MUKUNDA	: You are great, O boy. Cheers to your sense of duty. But – I am a Kshatriya, a warrior. – Should I flee like a burglar, like a timid one?
GOLAP	: No, never.
MUKUNDA	: Then?
GOLAP	: *(takes out a weapon and presents before him.)* Please, accept it, O King, without which a warrior like you is so miserable.
MUKUNDA	: You are a true warrior, O Boy, as you have truly understood the mind of a warrior and relieved him of his want. *(picks up the weapon.)* Come my dear, sword. You are the strength of a warrior – the only means of strength of a Kshatriya. *(puts a kiss on it.)*

GOLAP	:	My time is over, O king, footsteps of the guards are being heard from a distance. (*Exit.*)

(*Two guards enter.*)

GUARD I	:	What is it? The prisoner is free! He has a sword in his hand! Brothers! – Brothers! – Hurry up! – Hurry up!
MUKUNDA	:	You need not fear, guards. The prisoner is free but not fleeing.
GUARD II	:	What do you look at? – Catch hold of him. – Take the sword out.
MUKUNDA	:	You cannot – as long as I am alive. (*A scuffle ensues and the guards flee.*)
MUKUNDA	:	Now my path is clear.

(*Kalapahad enters.*)

KALAPAHAD	:	But you are now face to face with Kalapahad. Your hopes are futile. – Vain hope!
MUKUNDA	:	Still hopeful. I feel like enjoying an uphill task.
KALAPAHAD	:	So much arrogance!

(*They fight. Katalu and soldiers enter and assist Kalapahad:*)

MUKUNDA	:	(*Sword breaks while fighting.*) What to do now? Oh, Lord Jagannath, my only refuge!

(*Suddenly Golap enters with another sword.*)

GOLAP	:	Victory to Lord Jagannath! Please take another sword. (*Offers a sword.*)
KALAPAHAD	:	What is it? This is GOLAP : Traitor!
MUKUNDA	:	Fight! – Fight!

(*They again fight. Mukunda Dev defeats all and exits.*)

GOLAP	:	Cheers, gallant Mukunda Dev! – Victory to Lord Jagannath!

KALAPAHAD: Catch him – Chase him. (*A few soldiers pursued Mukunda.*) How surprising! Mukunda Dev alone defeated us all and disappeared.

KATALU. It is all for this boy only. – For this boy only, O the servant of Allah.

GOLAP : (*To Katalu*) What were you doing then? – Silently watching?

KALAPAHAD: (*angrily*) Meanest of mankind! Traitor! Is this the recompense of my affection? Is this the reward of my shelter to you?

GOLAP : This servant has only done his duty, Your Highness.

KALAPAHAD: By betraying the master?

GOLAP : By preserving the righteousness of the master, Your Highness.

KALAPAHAD: It's my spiritual duty to kill Hindus.

GOLAP : It's anti-religious.

KALAPAHAD: May be for you.

GOLAP : It's for the world, Your Highness.

KALAPAHAD: But not for me.

GOLAP : Don't you belong to this world?

KALAPAHAD: Nay. No need.

GOLAP : What is the need of shedding Hindu blood then?

KALAPAHAD: It's more necessary than chatting with you. Who is there? Arrest this traitor. I shall fulfil my promise by first shedding the blood of this Hindu with my own hands.

KTALU. Let's see what this young man is doing now. (*trying to catch Golap.*)

GOLAP : Beware, you traitor, you dog! Your Highness,

there is no need of anybody. This slave shall gladly carry out the orders of his master.

KALAPAHAD: (*Aside*) Oh, my heart, why are you getting tender? Be hard. – Harder than stone. O Mercy! O Love! You are all traitors. – I have no relationship with you any longer. Be off from me immediately. O Violence! O Hostility! Come to my heart. I am arranging a seat for you in it. Gladly have a seat. – I shall offer you Hindu blood – Hindu kingdom – Hindu religion as oblation. (*Aloud*) Get ready, O traitor. (*picks up a sword*)

GOLAP : I'm ready, My Lord! (*kneels down*) Lord Jagannath! Bless my master. Give shelter to this wretched soul.

KALAPAHAD: Surprising! Eh boy! No – (*raises his sword but it falls off his hand*) What's the matter? – Why did the sword fall off my hand? – Why does my whole being tremble? – Why does the whole earth tremble? – Why does the sky tremble? – The whole world is trembling! – Why this weakness? – Why does Kalapahad become so weak? Why this affection for a boy – a mere page? Impossible! – Who is there? Give me my sword. My sword. – My sword. – (*Katalu hands him a sword.*) I want Hindu blood. Hindu flesh. Destruction of Hindus. (*raises his sword*)

GOLAP : Give me a final glimpse of you, O Lord. (*Kalapahad and Golap look at each other as if in a trance and the sword falls off Kalapahad's hand.*)

(*Curtain*)

ACT IV
SCENE I
Camp in the Battle Field.
(*Mukunda Dev and his Body Guards are present.*)

MUKUNDA	: Guards, I have regained my lost strength. – Leave me, I shall go to the battle field.
GUARD	: O Monarch, cast a glance at yourself.
MUKUNDA	: Look at me! – Look at me while I have work to do! – Is it possible for a Kshatriya? It's impossible for Mukunda.
GUARD	: Shikhi and Manai are managing the war well.
MUKUNDA	: Can I be at rest depending on Shikhi and Manai? Can I depend on these two irresponsible idiots and be at peace? Alas! – Had they arrived in right time you would not have seen me in this bloody condition. We could have by now courted the Goddess of Victorious without loss of lives. Leave me. – Give me my sword. – I can't any longer put up with delay. (*tumult in the background*) – Where? – Where is my sword? (*rises up excitedly and snatches away a sword from the Guard.*)
MUKUNDA	: Victory to Lord Jagannath! (*Voice from the background: Victory to Lord Jagannath!*) This is the voice of our soldiers. Have they won or been defeated? (*Shikhi, Manai and soldiers enter.*)
SHIKHI	: We are victorious, Your Majesty. Please, have a look at the enemy camp. Mark, how

		the white flag is begging for peace with outstretched hands.
MANAI	:	Please have another look at this side. You can see how our esteemed enemy is approaching your venerable feet with slow steps and lowered heads to beg for truce.
MUKUNDA	:	*(aside)* Surprising! How was Kalapahad so quickly vanquished? *(aloud)* – Glory to my companions. – The glory be to my soldiers. – This glory is possible only for you. I am victorious now.

(Kalapahad enters.)

KALAPAHAD:		Greetings, Your Highness!
MUKUNDA	:	Hello, Commander!
KALAPAHAD:		The glory be to you! The glory be to your prowess, your skillfulness! In Bharatvarsha, I have rarely seen such a warrior, who cares a fig for his body, seldom cares for his life and engages himself in the battle alone like a ferocious lion against a horde of enemy soldiers. The most powerful Emperor Akbar has accepted defeat from you. It is not a panegyric of a sycophant. – It is my own observation – my assessment.
MUKUNDA	:	O Warrior! You are the suitable person for the epithets you have attributed to this humble soul. It's no exaggeration to mention that a warrior like you can hardly be found not only in India but also in the whole world. I can now clearly understand why Emperor Akbar was not content to invite me to supress your rebellion and had sent Katalu with a large army to support me.

SHIKHI	:	Thank God; a warrior now meets another warrior – A gem has met gold.
ALL	:	Victory to Emperor Mukunda Dev! Victory to Commander Kalapahad!
MUKUNDA	:	Victory to Emperor Akbar of Delhi!
ALL	:	Victory to Emperor Akbar of Delhi!
KALAPAHAD	:	Please come Emperor, let me entertain you as my guest today.
MUKUNDA	:	First of all, let the documents of treaty be drafted, signed and sent to emperor Akbar. Well, Commander! Before the documents are drafted, you have to surrender Traitor Katalu to me. – Emperor of Delhi must like to see the head of this meanest of mankind before he listens to the terms of the truce.
SHIKHI	:	Katalu has been killed, Emperor.
MUKUNDA	:	Katalu has been killed! Where is his severed head?
SHIKHI	:	His dead body has vanished.
MUKUNDA	:	How is it so? (*aside*) I doubt.
SHIKHI	:	I looked into the matter and found that for fear of his execution some of his faithful followers have buried Katalu's dead body somewhere.
MUKUNDA	:	(*aside*) I can't believe it. I have to look into the matter myself.

(*A messenger from Delhi enters.*)

MESSENGER	:	Victory to king Mukunda Deb!
MUKUNDA	:	What is the news from Delhi, messenger? Come, let's go into this camp.

(*Exit messenger.*)

	Shikhi and Manai, escort the Commander honourably into my spacious camp. (*Exit Mukunda Deb.*)
SHIKHI	: Nawab Saheb, what do you guess about the purpose of the messenger's visit?
KALAPAHAD:	Perhaps, to know the outcome of the war.
SHIKHI	: Yes, that might be one of the reasons. Can attending the grand birthday celebration of the Badshah be another reason?
MANAI	: Then our job will be done without bloodshed.
KALAPAHAD:	We need not be express our happiness depending on our guess. Now let's move to the appropriate place. Someone may doubt us if we are seen here talking. Our secret counselling should be done secretly with all care.
SHIKHI	: Let's go, Nawab Saheb.
MANAI	: (*aside*) Ah! When shall Manai Mahanty be crowned with the title of Commander? (*All Exit.*) (*Curtain*)

SCENE II
Forest.

(*Golap enters in the guise of a monk.*)

GOLAP : I am very happy today though staying in the forest in exile. I'm very glad that I have saved my lord from the sins of homicide. I have saved the life of the holy king. But I cannot rest in peace until the war has come to an end and until the holy king has not left this place.

	(*Firoja enters.*)
FIROJA	: There is no way to be content, Golap.
GOLAP	: Why? What's the matter, Firoja? What's the news of the war?
FIROJA	: Truce has been accorded. Mukunda Dev has been to Delhi to participate in the birthday celebration of the Badshah.
GOLAP	: It's good news, Firoja.
FIROJA	: It might have been good news if the assistants of Mukunda Dev had not betrayed him.
GOLAP	: What betrayal?
FIROJA	: According to the terms of the truce, Mukunda Dev has commanded his assistants to take out all the weapons from the Muslim soldiers to ensure peace in the kingdom. But as soon as the departed, they have taken away all the weapons from our soldiers and sent the Muslim soldiers to our kingdom with all the weapons. – My friend was telling that the truce is only hypocrisy. The real intention of the Nawab is to send Mukunda Dev away by all means and carry out his devilish oath.
GOLAP	: What Lord Jagannath wills is known to Him only. Well Firoja, couldn't Mukunda Dev, being a shrewd statesman, make out the hypocrisy of the enemy?
FIROJA	: When did he get leisure to see through the betrayal of the enemy? The invitation of the Badshah spoiled everything.
GOLAP	: What can be done now, Firoja? Will the Nawab indulge in such heinous work as

	long as we are alive? Will he be in hell?
FIROJA	: What Allah, the Almighty, wishes, Golap!
GOLAP	: Whatever might be the wish of Allah, the Almighty, we shall do our duty.
FIROJA	: Come Golap, our friend is waiting for us. (*Both of them are about to leave.*)
GOLAP	: Look Firoja, two people are coming in this direction. They seem to be known to us.
FIROJA	: These are Katalu and Rahamat. How could Katalu survive? It was announced that he was dead.
GOLAP	: Rahamat was thrown into prison, wasn't he?
FIROJA	: Some days before it was rumoured that he had escaped the prison. A poor guard was executed for that.
GOLAP	: Katalu should have been executed instead. Look, they are coming towards us. It can be guessed from their gestures that they are busy in some conspiration. Let's hide ourselves and listen to them. (*Katalu and Rahamat enter.*)
KATALU	: Rahamat, if Allah wishes we can fulfil our desires.
RAHAMAT	: How?
KATALU	: You have heard from the messenger that I shall be the chief assistant of Kalapahad during our invasion of Odisha.
RAHAMAT	: Yes, I have heard.
KATALU	: What more! I shall be Kalapahad's confidant. With this opportunity I shall remove your obstacle.
RAHAMAT	: Bah! Very Good!

KATALU	:	Moreover, when Mukunda Dev comes to know that Kalapahad has betrayed him and returned to Odisha, he will hurriedly return there.
RAHAMAT	:	What will happen then?
KATALU	:	You will convince him that you will help him and thus you will remove my obstacle.
FIROJA	:	(*in hiding*) Ah, Allah!
RAHAMAT	:	(*puzzled*) Who? Whose voice is it? (*flees towards the jungle*)
KATALU	:	Surely an enemy. Kill him immediately. He has heard all our secret plans. (*flees*) (*Firoja and Golap hurriedly enter.*)
FIROJA	:	Golap, Help me. Help me.
GOLAP	:	Firoja, Remember Allah. He will rescue us. (*Golap is ready to fight. Katalu and Rahamat hurriedly enter.*)
KATALU	:	Here is the enemy.
RAHAMAT	:	This is Firoja.
KATALU	:	Finish her, Rahamat. Delay may be ominous.
GOLAP	:	Firoja, stay calmly behind me. – You need not fear as long as I am alive.
RAHAMAT	:	Bah! How courageous the rustic is!
GOLAP	:	Fight me, oh, the meanest of mankind. (*Golap's beard falls off while fighting.*)
KATALU	:	This is Golap. Kill him, Rahamat. He is a very dangerous boy. (*Golap's sword breaks while fighting.*)
FIROJA	:	It's the end this time. Oh Allah! (*collapses.*) (*Golap recedes to the background while fighting.*)
GOLAP	:	Lord Jagannath, save the life of Firoja.
KATALU	:	Surrender your weapons, boy.

RAHAMAT	: Behold hell this time. (*Several arrows shot at Rahamat and Katalu and pierce them.*)
RAHAMAT & KATALU	: Uh! (*Both collapse to the ground.*) (*Hunters enter.*)
HUNTERS	: Eh, these are not boars; these are two human beings. Flee. - Flee. (*Hunters exit.*)
GOLAP	: Oh God! You are indeed the Lord of the poor. Get up, Firoja. See, how benevolent Allah is! How He has saved us from the enemies!
FIROJA	: You are great, Allah. Thank you for Your mercy. (*Both exit.*) (*Curtain*)

SCENE III
Royal Chamber.

DULIA	: Alas, father. Today is your birthday. What a grand celebration there might have been! What great merriment there might have been for me! But where are all these? Only bitter cries rent the air. Tear prevails everywhere. Who has wrought this scene? Who has caused this sad cry? Rahamat, the devil! Uh, he has fled. He is free from suffering. Is the Lord just in this? (*Golap enters.*)
GOLAP	: The Lord is just, sister.
DULIA	: Because the prisoner has escaped?
GOLAP	: No, for being sent to hell.
DULIA	: Is escape from prison like going to hell?
GOLAP	: It has been perhaps like that in case of Rahamat.

DULIA	: Is it a joke, Golap?
GOLAP	: Dare I joke with the Begum? See, Nawab is coming. Listen to everything from him. Let me go into hiding. (*Exit Golap.*)

(*Kalapahad and Firoja enter.*)

KALAPAHAD:	Is Katalu also killed Firoja?
FIROJA	: Both of them at the same time, Your Highness.
DULIA	: Who is the other Firoja?
FIROJA	: That devil, Rahamat, the murderer of your brother.
DULIA	: Rahamat! Thank God.
KALAPAHAD:	Oh! Is Katalu, my chief assistant, killed? Mukunda's chief enemy is killed – What can be done now?
FIROJA	: Your Majesty, why are you so much sad for Katalu? He is a traitor. He too was scheming against you.
KALAPAHAD:	Against me? Leave it; I have to get ready now.
DULIA	: Thank God. Both the traitors ae killed at the same time, Golap.
KALAPAHAD:	Where is Golap?
DULIA	: (*biting her teeth*) How can she be here? She has been banished.
KALAPAHAD:	(*heaving a deep sigh*) Lovely boy! Well, I have to proceed towards Odisha today by any means. Need I fear? Instead, I have got Shikhi and Manai, two of Mukunda's chief enemies, to help me.
DULIA	: Oh, Lord of my Life! Desist from attacking Odisha. The Hindus shall be penalised for the wrongs they have done. Look at the

	incident of Katalu and Rahamat. Allah shall punish the sinner.
KALAPAHAD:	Ha! Ha! The Deity of my Life! Have you ever seen Allah? Has He got limbs like us? Does He have strength to work like us?
DULIA	: Whether he has strength to work or not, whether he has limbs or not, I have staunch faith that He exists.
KALAPAHAD:	Illusion! A great illusion! If He exists He is a lifeless lump. He has no strength to work. We are the doers. Leave it; I need not reason about it. I have to get ready immediately. I shall carry out my promise. Hindu's blood – Hindu's flesh – Hindu's ruin! (*Hurriedly exit.*)
DULIA	: Golap! Brother! (*Golap enters.*)
GOLAP	: Begum! Sister!
DULIA	: What is the way out now?
DULIA	: Lord Jagannath will look after all.
DULIA	: Certainly, Lord Jagannath will find some way out. I could have killed only one traitor, Rahamat. But to kill both the traitors at a time can only be done by Lord Jagannath. Could anybody else have done that? He is our only refuge now.
GOLAP	: Certainly, He will convey the way for us to follow.
DULIA	: Sing Golap, sing a song in praise of glory of the Lord. Let us be delighted with the song.
GOLAP	: (*Sings.*) (Song)

O Enchanter of the universe,
O redeemer of the downtrodden,
O Lord Jagannath,
Thy name is holy nectar.
Drink this holy nectar,
O Lord's beloved,
With disregard to caste or creed.
Allah is He, He is Jesus, Buddha and Krishna as well,
He is pleased in whatever way one chants His name,
O brothers, never ever indulge in pointless quarrel,
Pray for his blessings, peace and Heaven.
See, Nawab is coming here. (*Exit Golap.*)
    (*Kalapahad enters.*)

KALAPAHAD: Who was singing? Dulia? It seemed to be Golap's voice.

DULIA : Are you dreaming of Golap, My Lord?

KALAPAHAD: Day in and day out Golap comes to my dream. Although a page, he had prevailed over my stony heart. I still feel for her, as if I am her – Leave it, I have very good news for you, the Deity of my heart.

DULIA : What good news, My Lord?

KALAPAHAD: Ramachandra Bhanja has sent his messengers, Shikhi and Manai, with the message that he is going to help me.

DULIA : Who is that devil?

KALAPAHAD: Not a devil, he is the Chief of Saranga Garh, and a subordinate ruler of Mukunda Deb.

DULIA : My Lord! –

KALAPAHAD: No, I don't seek your counsel. My soldiers are ready. I have to proceed now. Farewell.

DULIA : Now?

KALAPAHAD: O, yes, just now. (*Exit.*)
DULIA : (*sighs*) Allah! What to do now? My Lord – (*Golap enters.*)
FIROJA : Did you hear everything, Golap?
GOLAP : No need to worry, Firoja. I have told you that he is doing his duty, we too should do our duty.
FIROJA : Can we succeed?
GOLAP : Possibly, through self-sacrifice.
FIROJA : We are ready for that every moment.
GOLAP : Only suicide is not the answer. We have to make ourselves ready in such a way, and we have to perform such tasks which is nearly impossible for a tender woman. It should be a miracle.
(*Dressed as a warrior, Dulia enters.*)
DULIA : I am going to perform that miracle, Golap.
FIROJA : What is this apparel, Begum Saheb?
DULIA : This kind of apparel is needed now. Go Firoja, dress up like me. Eh, brother, do you like this gear?
GOLAP : Very much, sister. It is now the will of God. This gear is now necessary to carry out the task of Lord Jagannath. Come, Firoja, let's dress up similarly and work for the Lord – help dharma.
ALL : Allah, Hu Akbar! Victory to Lord Jagannath! (*All exit heroically.*)
(*Curtain*)

SCENE IV
Hilly forest.

QUEEN : Soldiers, the enemy is fast approaching. Once again, shout "Victory to Lord Jagannath" drowning the skies. Quietly station yourselves at the opposite side of the hill.

GENERAL : What kind of command is it, Honourable Queen?

QUEEN : There is no time to explain, General.

GENERAL : As you please, Honourable Queen.

ALL : "Victory to Lord Jagannath". "Victory to King Mukunda Deb."
(*Soldiers hurriedly exit.*)
(*Background Voice. "Allah Hu Akbar". "Victory to Kalapahad".*)

QUEEN : Our slogan is rightly responded. Let's now stay in hiding. (*The Queen hurriedly exits.*)
(*Kalapahad along with his soldiers hurriedly enters.*)

KALAPAHAD: I have now got the view of the enemy. (*looking around*) Where is the enemy? I can't see anybody here? Where does this sound come from then? Soldiers, have a look at this direction.

SOLDIERS : We are too weak to walk, Nawab. Uh, we are very thirsty.

KALAPAHAD: (*aside*) I too have the same fate. (*heaving a deep sigh*) What is the way out? What a blunder I have committed! Why did we pursue the enemy by following their sound without the knowledge of the road? Why did I venture to do it without consulting

		Shikhi and Manai? They might be waiting there in that field.
SOLDIERS	:	It's unbearable for us, Nawab Saheb. *(Some sit down and a few lie down due to exhaustion.)*
KALAPAHAD:		What a crisis! *(Background Voice. "Victory to Lord Jagannath".)*
KALAPAHAD:		The same sound again! *(listening intently)* Where does this sound come from? *(The Queen along with the soldiers enters.)* Here is the enemy. Soldiers! What a figure! Is it the Goddess Chandi out for a battle?
QUEEN	:	Soldiers, attack!
KALAPAHAD:		Rise up, warriors! The enemy has appeared before you. Get up; pick up your weapons. *(Soldiers try to get up.)*
SOLDIERS OF UTKAL	:	Kill them! – Kill them! – We have a good opportunity.
QUEEN	:	Halt. The enemy is tired – without weapons – completely unprepared too. Allow them a little time to get ready.
SOLDIERS OF UTKAL	:	Your Highness!
QUEEN	:	Refrain from attack.
MUSLIM SOLDIERS	:	When you have allowed us a little time, please grant us life to complete your kindness. Give us a little water. We are very thirsty, mother, very thirsty.
QUEEN	:	Soldiers, satisfy the desires of the thirsty.
GENERAL	:	They are our enemies, Your Highness.
QUEEN	:	Now they are not our foes, Commander.

MUSLIM SOLDIERS	:	Oh, intense thirst! We are dying.
QUEEN	:	Give, General, give water to the thirsty, food to the hungry. Save the lives of the dying. It's not the time to make distinction between the friends and foes.
GENERAL	:	We are almost running out of food and water.
QUEEN	:	Freely distribute the food we have without any hesitation.
MUSLIM SOLDIERS	:	Mother, who are you? You have appeared before us like a goddess in the guise of a mortal. Your words are like nectar that quenches our hunger and thirst.

(*Soldiers of Utkal distribute food and water.*)

KALAPAHAD:		Ah, me! What do I see? Oh, my heart! What peace do you enjoy?
QUEEN	:	Now, you are perhaps ready for the battle.
KALAPAHAD:		Battle?
QUEEN	:	Are you surprised?
KALAPAHAD:		Battle with the Giver of Life!
QUEEN	:	Aren't you warriors? Don't you know the rules of the war?
KALAPAHAD:		We don't need to. A son is never ashamed if we are defeated by the mother who has given us life.

(*Ramachandra, Shikhi and Manai enter.*)

RAMA	:	But I do feel ashamed, Nawab Saheb. Is it the way of fulfilling your promise? Is it the way you honour a promise to your friend? Being the greatest warrior, how do you bow down to a woman? Shikhi and Manai,

what prowess did you see with Kalapahad that you had invited me to help him?

KALAPAHAD: (*aside*) I am indeed too enchanted to neglect my duties. – Destruction, total destruction! –Destruction of Mukunda Deb! – Destruction of Hindus! – (*aloud*) Raja Saheb, forgive me. I lost my sense of duty owing to a little weakness of mine. I now thank you since you have made me conscious. Soldiers, destroy the enemy. (*Looking at the Queen*) What are you staring at me for? I am ready to fight.

QUEEN : No, you are not ready. You are not ready as an enemy. – You are a friend. I now see that the enemy has become a friend.

RAMA : Do you know Queen who is the guide, the mastermind in this regard?

SHIKHI : If you do not know —

MANAI : Then, listen to me.

QUEEN : You traitors!

RAMA : We are not traitors, Queen, your Mukunda Deb is the traitor.

QUEEN : Only a traitor can say such a thing.

RAMA : A traitor's wife can say such a thing.

QUEEN : Liar!

RAMA : Liar! Ha! Ha! (*laughs*) By what law has Mukunda Deb usurped the freedom of Saranga Garh, Queen? By what rule has he considered this independent king inferior to a subordinate servant?

QUEEN : Of course, it's your rebellious attitude, traitor.

RAMA : How? In what way?

QUEEN	:	The way I see you now – as everybody has seen you.
RAMA	:	How dare you! Being a mere woman! It may be decided now who is just?
QUEEN	:	Listen to me, O the soldiers of the Holy King, the Holy King is absent now. His subordinate king and the nobles are rebels. Your leader is only a woman. In this case, you can decide your course of action and perform your duty accordingly.
SOLDIERS OF UTKAL	:	We will fight for Mukunda Deb.
QUEEN	:	Victory to King Mukunda Deb!
RAMA	:	Dwellers of Saranga Garh, is it your opinion? Will you fight on the side of injustice?
SOLDIER I	:	I don't know what is justice or otherwise. We will sacrifice our lives for one who has fed and educated us.
KALAPAHAD	:	You need not fear, O Ramachandra Deb. Henceforth you are the ruler of Odisha. (*laughs*)
QUEEN	:	Soldiers, advance. Utter the name of Lord Jagannath and advance on the path of your duty.
SOLDIERS OF UTKAL	:	Victory to Lord Jagannath! Victory to king Mukunda Deb!
MUSLIM SOLDIERS	:	Allah hu Akbar! Victory to Nawab Kalapahad! Victory to King Ramachandra Deb! (*An intense fight ensues. Soldiers of Utkal recede.*) (*Background Voice : Allah hu Akbar!*)

QUEEN	: Fight, soldiers! Don't retreat. Don't tarnish the name of Utkal. Don't tarnish the name of Odia nationality. Die for your duty. Victory or loss is in the hands of destiny.
BACKGROUND VOICE	: Allah hu Akbar! Victory to Nawab Kalapahad! Victory to King Ramachandra Deb!
QUEEN	: "Victory to King Ramachandra Deb!" It's unbearable to hear it as long as I live. (*Hurriedly exit.*)
MUSLIM SOLDIERS	: (*Hurriedly enter.*) What a ferocious woman! O Allah!

(*Hurriedly exit.*)
(*Curtain*)

SCENE V
The Bank of the Tank Inside the Fort.

(*The Queen enters with the head of Ramachandra.*)

QUEEN	: Ha! Ha! Ha! (*laughs*) Jackal! Giving airs before the lioness in the absence of the lion! You have reaped its consequences. I don't need your head any longer. It's a sin to touch the head of a traitor like you. Go, roll in this dry field until you are feasted on by the carnivorous beasts. (*throwing the head away*) Others shall have the same fate. (*A soldier enters.*)
1st SOLDIER	: It's all destroyed, Your Highness.
QUEEN	: What destruction, Soldier?
1st SOLDIER	: The Muslims have again come back.
QUEEN	: Why do you fear? Fight again. (*2nd Soldier hurriedly enters.*)

2nd SOLDIER : We are vanquished, Great Queen.
QUEEN : Aren't you ashamed to utter 'vanquished'? This Odia tongue shall utter 'victory' or be silent for good.
(*3rd Soldier enters.*)
3rd SOLDIER : Our General is dead, Great Queen.
QUEEN : Is the General dead? O Lord Jagannath! What message I did receive! There is nothing to fear about, soldiers. You needn't fear as long as I am alive. Move forward – Fight – Either be victorious or court death.
(*As they advance, the women of the city enter.*)
CITY WOMEN: Greet Queen, the enemy is inside the fort. Defeat the enemy and make them retreat or else enter on our dead bodies.
(*Kalapahad enters.*)
KALAPAHAD: Shall we enter on your dead body? So disdainful! Why are you so arrogant, only because you have beheaded a rat?
QUEEN : Kalapahad! You perhaps do not know what a Kshatriya woman does when she has to surrender.
KALAPAHAD: I know quite well, lady. Try to test it. Soldiers, arrest these women.
(*Soldiers advance.*)
QUEEN : I warn you, rats.
(*Muslim Soldiers are overawed by her radiance.*)
KALAPAHAD: Don't hesitate. – Step forward. – Torture them. – Take revenge. – Finish Hindus. – All Hindus.
(*Soldiers swing their weapons.*)
QUEEN : Sisters, the clear water of this tank is our last refuge.

KALAPAHAD: Surround the tank, soldiers.
(*Background Voice:* "*All finished*". "*All finished*")
KALAPAHAD: What is it? What ruination!
(*Shikhi and Manai hurriedly enter.*)
SHIKHI : Three strange youth have burnt down our camp filled with food and armaments. They have massacred a half of our exhausted soldiers.
KALAPAHAD: And you have quietly witnessed the scene without doing anything and then came running to me to inform that, haven't you?
MANAI : Nawab Saheb. If you look at their radiant demeanour and enthusiasm, you will feel they were not three but three hundred – three thousand. Listen to sad screams. Look at that rising fire.
KALAPAHAD: What an astounding loss!
MUSLIM SOLDIERS : "Allah hu Akbar".
(*All hurriedly exit.*)
QUEEN : What news! Has Lord Jagannath appeared to rescue us along with his brother and sister?
(*Background Voice. "Allah hu Akbar".*)
QUEEN : This is the joyous victory shouts of the Muslims! Are the youths defeated then? No, this might be only a pretext of Lord Jagannath to save our honour. Sisters, we needn't delay. Let's immerse our body in this holy tank before it is touched by the Muslims.
CITY WOMEN: Jaya Maa Bhagabati. (*Jump into the pond.*)
(*Background Voice : Jaya Jagannath!*)

QUEEN	:	(*heaving a sigh*) Mocking! Mocking in the name of Lord Jagannath! See Muslims, how many are left to be imprisoned by you? (*Dulia, Golap and Firoja enter.*)
DULIA	:	Where is the Queen?
QUEEN	:	In the waters of this tank, O Muslims.
GOLAP	:	Queen! Queen! (*coming closer*)
QUEEN	:	(*aside*) O Lord of my life, we won't meet in this life. My fears have come true. This is my only prayer, Lord Jagannath, may my lord be victorious and safeguard the freedom of the nation or gladly depart to Heaven while fighting.
DULIA	:	Queen! Queen! Please halt. I am Dulia.
GOLAP	:	I am Golap.
FIROJA	:	I am Firoja.
QUEEN	:	Oh, you! Why are you in the attire of the warriors?
DULIA	:	To support the Queen who has given us refuge.
QUEEN	:	You have done a lot, sisters. It is only because of you our honour is safe. Thank you. I should not delay. (*Background Voice. Allah Hu Akbar!*)
QUEEN	:	Listen to the tumultuous noise of the enemies. Farewell! Farewell! (*jumps into water*) (*Kalapahad, Shikhi and Manai along with the soldiers hurriedly enter.*)
KALAPAHAD:		Where is the Queen?
DULIA	:	Inside this tank. (*All quietly look at the tank with surprise and Golap etc. disappear.*) (*Curtain*)

ACT V
SCENE I

In front of the Temple of Goddess Biraja.
(Background Voice : "Allah Hu Akbar")
(Mukunda Deb hurriedly enter.)

MUKUNDA : Soldiers, wake up! You can hear the chirping of birds in the morning as well as the battle cries of the enemies. Give up laziness. Say good bye to night and sleepiness.

SOLDIERS: *(enter hurriedly)* Victory to Lord Jagannath! Victory to Gajapati Mukunda Deb!

(Background Voice. "Allah Hu Akbar". "Victory to Kalapahad!")

MUKUNDA : It's intolerable. Come soldiers, uttering the name of the Goddess, let's join the today's battle. May this day carry the message of our victory to other states or be turned into eternal night at the sight of our dead bodies!

SOLDIERS : Victory to Gajapati Mukunda Deb!

MUKUNDA : *(advancing)* What a terrible sight! What humiliation! Maa, why is this miserable condition? Where is the decorated arch of your temple? Where are the beautiful images carved on the temple walls? What destruction! Oh, what a horrible sight! Here is one image without hands and feet – There the stone remains of an idol – and somewhere an image has totally vanished. – Kalapahad! What havoc have you wrought?

(Shikhi and Manai along with the soldiers enter.)

SHIKHI : It is not complete yet, O Raja Saheb.

MANAI	: It may not be complete even with Shree Mandir.
MUKUNDA	: It will be complete with your death, traitors.
MANAI	: (*laughing*) In our death or in yours?
SHIKHI	: Your death is certain, Raja Saheb. Your loyal Kony Singh, for whose special favours we are called traitors, has departed to the other world. Your loving dear queen for whom your heart might be throbbing with joy every moment at the prospect of meeting her is no more.
MUKUNDA	: Queen is no more! (*pause*)
SOLDIER	: The great Queen is no more, O King.
MUKUNDA	: Wake up, Mukunda. Wake up, soldiers. Proceed on the path of your duty. It is not the time for lament. Traitors, you very well know, how much strength Mukunda Deb wields in his arms – how dexterously he uses his weapons.
SHIKHI	: We are prepared for that, O King.
MUKUNDA	: Attack soldiers. (*Fight ensues. Muslim soldiers retreat. Shikhi and Manai collapse.*) Traitors, take your due rewards. (*about to kill*) No. I will not stain my sword with the blood of mean fellows like you. It's also not your fit punishment. Your punishment is that you should be shorn of your limbs like these disfigured images. Soldiers, imprison these meanest of mankind and throw them into the prison camp. (*Soldiers exit with the prisoners.*) My Dear, how much I wished to behold you on my return from

Delhi. How can I know that my loyal soldiers shall turn out so disloyal? This happens when the enemy is sly.
(*A guard enters.*)

GUARD : A messenger has come from Cuttack, O Great King.

MUKUNDA : We shall hear the secret news about the enemies. (*All exit.*)

(*Curtain*)

SCENE II

The Camp of Mukunda.
(*Mukunda Deb and the Messenger enter.*)

MUKUNDA : Tell me, messenger, let me be glorified by listening to it again. O Queen, I don't regret for being separated from you. You are the right consort of a warrior. You have performed the right duty of a consort in the absence of your husband and departed to the other world. What a traitor Ramachandra is! Messenger!

MESSENGER : Yes, Your Highness. It's for him only we are passing through this misfortune.

MUKUNDA : Ramachandra! You, being a denizen of the state, have ruined the state. Why didn't you take revenge against me, if you had any personal antagonism against me? You flooded the kingdom with the blood of the innocent subjects. You have surrendered the freedom, which is the most precious wealth, the supreme glory, and the most venerable thing of the kingdom, to the enemy. Above all, you have made *Sanatan Dharma*, the

	pride of the Hindus and their prized wealth, a plaything for the enemies. Go, messenger, command the soldiers on my behalf to get ready. I shall immediately proceed to war. I can hardly tolerate the humiliation meted out to the kingdom and the religion.
MESSENGER :	Your Majesty, it's now night. Can't we wait till the morning?
MUKUNDA :	Waiting till the morning? Such a long time! Intolerable! Carry out my orders immediately. (*Messenger exits.*) Kalapahad! You were also a Hindu once. You were following the religion sincerely. What are you doing now? Your chief goal is to destroy Hindu religion. Oh! (*Tired soldiers enter.*) Oh, the soldiers have come. Soldiers, I will start for the war just now. Are you ready?
1st SOLDIER :	(*showing fatigue*) Your command shall be carried out, O Great King.
MUKUNDA :	What is it? I don't see your enthusiasm and eagerness. Why?
1st SOLDIER :	We feel very exhausted, O Great King.
MUKUNDA :	Exhaustion!
1st SOLDIER :	Till the morn –
MUKUNDA :	Do you want rest? Rest, rest ... (*laughing*) Ha! Ha! Go, court eternal rest as you wish. (*aside*) I too don't know why I am so tired.
SOLDIERS :	We are ready, O Great King.
MUKUNDA :	No, no, go and take rest. Your King too prays for rest. (*All exit.*) (*Shikhi and Manai with a knife in hand quietly enter.*)

SHIKHI	: Brother, be quiet.
MANAI	: Let's see, where he is sleeping.
SHIKHI	: Keep quiet. I am checking.
MANAI	: I hear him snoring. Bah! Bah! He is soundly asleep. Let me extinguish the fire of pain in me with my own hands.
SHIKHI	: No, brother, allow the killer to murder. His aim is unerring. His heart is steady. See how the knife is firmly fixed in my fist after drinking the blood of the guards.
MANAI	: Brother, why these looks?
SHIKHI	: Silence. (*They exit.*)

(*Mukunda Dev's voice is heard from the background* : Oh, I am dying. Lord Jagannath, may your wish be fulfilled.)

(Curtain)

SCENE III
A Road in the city of Puri.

(*Some citizens enter.*)

1st CITIZEN	: Brother, let's go away. We can't stay here any longer.
2nd CITIZEN	: Well brother, please wait a little. Let me collect the gold and silver I have at home.
1st CITIZEN	: Very fine. Go and surrender your life too.
2nd CITIZEN	: Surrender my life? Surrender my precious life? Then I don't need them. Let's flee.
3rd CITIZEN	: I have left behind my children at home.
1st CITIZEN	: What can you do then? They will meet their fate. Let's survive first.

(Background Voice. Allah Hu Akbar. Victory to Nawab Kalapahad.)

ALL	:	Oh brothers, here comes Kalapahad, pulling down the iron fence.
		(*While fleeing, Dulia, Golap and Firoja enter.*)
GOLAP	:	Halt, brothers.
ALL	:	Greetings, Mr. Sepoy. Please, save our lives.
1st CITIZEN	:	Oh, Big bosses, take all my property but spare my life.
2nd CITIZEN	:	Oh, Great Lords, accept all my gold and silver. But spare my life.
3rd CITIZEN	:	Take my children, but spare me.
GOLAP	:	What did you say, brothers? For mere life, will you sacrifice your children to the enemies? How are you ready to surrender your humanity to the enemies? Fie on you. Are you humans or beasts in human form? You consider your own happiness as the ultimate happiness; your conscience is inert. As a consequence, you are prepared not only to bring ruin to yourself, but also to the nation and your religion. Fie on your manliness, on your life!
		(*Everybody looks at one another in bewilderment.*)
DULIA	:	Give up your fears, brothers. We are your friends.
ALL.		Friends! (*They look at Dulia with surprise.*)
DULIA	:	Yes, brothers. We are your friends. We seek your help.
1st CITIZEN	:	Help? We have nothing of our own.
DULIA	:	You have everything, brothers. You have strength in your body, courage in your heart, strong resolve of mind. We want these from you.

2nd CITIZEN	:	Great Lords, we have none of such things. Why are you forcing us into those troubles?
DULIA	:	Why? Are you blind or deaf? Look at your houses; they are on fire. Look at are your holy temples; they have been smashed into heaps of stones. Listen, how the pitiful screams of your children are rending the earth and tearing the skies. Wake up! Arise! Pick up arms.
ALL	:	Who are you that made us awake.? (*Background Voice. Allah Hu Akbar!*)
DULIA	:	Listen to the enemy's cheerful screams of victory. Come with whatever weapon you get and butcher the enemies.
GOLAP	:	Please, shout in one voice, "Victory to Lord Jagannath".
ALL	:	"Victory to Lord Jagannath".

(*All hurriedly exit.*)
(*Curtain*)

SCENE IV
Temple of Lord Jagannath at Puri.

(*Priests are standing with weapons.*)

1st PRIEST	:	Brother, there is no way out now. The Muslims are coming closer.
2nd PRIEST	:	Enemy soldiers are fast advancing like locusts. (*Background Voice. Allah Hu Akbar.*)
3rd PRIEST	:	Lord Jagannath! Please save Yourself. We have no strength to protect You. (*All are about to go away.*) (*Dulia, Golap and citizens enter.*)

DULIA	: You have enough strength, brothers. Utter the names of your cherished deities and be firm to do your duty to your God.
1st PRIEST	: Who are you? Are you sent by the Lord?
2nd PRIEST	: They must be sent by Lord Jagannath.
ALL	: Victory to Lord Jagannath.

(Background Voice. Allah Hu Akbar.)
(Kalapahad along with his soldiers enters.)

KALAPAHAD: Vain desire, Hindus. You cannot escape the poisonous bite of the trodden snake. Can you save your God from burning flames of anger? Look all around, all places have been turned into cremation grounds. The earth has been overburdened with the embrace of Hindu corpses. The sea has been red with the flow of Hindu blood into it. Listen, how the pitiable cries of Hindus have outdone the roars of the sea and echoed in the skies; how the devil is clapping his hands in the Hindu temples instead of the sounds of conch shells and brass bells. All vain desires!

1st PRIEST : Please spare us, Nawab Saheb. May you take away all we have, but leave this Temple.

KALAPAHAD: Shall I leave the Temple? Shall I leave the Temple for which the Brahmins have turned into *Chandals*, and conscientious humans have turned into devils?

GOLAP : Nawab Saheb, punish the miscreants. Why would you unnecessarily destroy the Temple?

KALAPAHAD: It is the punishment for wrongdoers.

DULIA : This the punishment for all Hindus.
KALAPAHAD: My target is Hindu's blood, Hindu's flesh and demolition of Hindu religion.
DULIA : Nawab Saheb!
KALAPAHAD: I don't want to listen to anything. I shall fulfil my promise. Break into the Temple, soldiers. Smash the image of every god and goddess. Snatch the image of Lord Jagannath, the supreme pride of the Hindus. Raze this Temple, the sculptural glory of the Hindu artisans, to ground.
GOLAP : As long as there is life in us, you cannot do it, Nawab Saheb.
KALAPAHAD: Preposterous! Fight me then. (*As fight begins, the priests and citizens flee.*) Now surrender yourselves, O young man.
GOLAP : Never. (*Fight ensues and being wounded Golap collapses.*)
KALAPAHAD: Give way, O Youngman. Come in, soldiers.
DULIA : You cannot as long as I am alive.
KALAPAHAD: You have seen the fate your friend. Why should you needlessly sacrifice your life?
GOLAP : (*still lying on the ground*) Brother, as long as you have strength in body and courage in heart, don't allow the soldiers to advance even a little space as the point a needle occupies.
DULIA : Brother, I promise, as long as I am alive, I shall obey you to the letter.
KALAPAHAD: No more excuse, soldiers, attack. (*Soldiers attack. Kalapahad inflicts wounds on Dulia and enters the temple.*)
(*Firoja enters.*)

FIROJA	:	Dear friend!
DULIA	:	*(lying on the ground)* Oh, I am dying! O Lord of my life! I'm very thirsty. Firoja, give me some water.
FIROJA	:	Golap, O Golap, see how miserable our friend is!
GOLAP	:	*(rising)* Sister! Sister!
DULIA	:	Oh, give me a little water, Golap. O Lord of my life!
GOLAP	:	Where are the soldiers? Some noise is audible. Firoja, hold our friend. This place is not safe for us.

(Golap and Firoja hold Dulia in their arms and exit.)
(Curtain)

SCENE V
The Sea Beach.

(A funeral pyre is burning. The Hindus frightfully stare at it. The Muslims delightfully hold the image of Lord Jagannath beside Kalapahad who is standing there.)

KALAPAHAD: Rise flames. — Burn ferociously. — You have chewed Hindu's bones. — You have drunk Hindu's blood. — Now, suck Hindu's bone marrow. — Your flames shall be content and my agony shall be pacified. Soldiers, fire is burning; flames are rising; throw the prize possession of the Hindus, their soul and this inert wood idol into fire. May, in no time, Hindu's wealth be burn to ashes! My heart's desire shall be fulfilled!

(Soldiers shout "Allah hu Akbar" and throw the image of Lord Jagannath into fire.)

HINDUS	:	Alas Jagannath! (*Golap hurriedly enters.*)
GOLAP	:	Don't cry in vain, useless ones. (*Golap jumps into fire and recovers the image of Lord Jagannath.*) I could save my Lord. Brothers, take our Lord away.
HINDUS	:	(*holding the Lord firmly*) Victory to Lord Jagannath! (*exit quickly*)
GOLAP	:	I can stand no more. (*sits down*)
KALAPAHAD	:	Who are you, strange boy?
GOLAP	:	My Lord!
KALAPAHAD	:	Golap!
GOLAP	:	(*removing her turban*) O Lord of my Life! (*collapses*)
KALAPAHAD	:	Who? Tilottama! Tilottama, the Deity of my Life! (*advancing towards her*)
TILOTTAMA	:	O Lord of my Life! This maid has finished her job. Bid me farewell.
KALAPAHAD	:	Bid you farewell?
TILOTTAMA	:	There is no way out.
KALAPAHAD	:	No way out?
TILOTTAMA	:	Give up futile thoughts, My Lord. If you do any favour to me, grant me peace.
KALAPAHAD	:	How can I grant you peace when my heart is without it!
TILOTTAMA	:	Give up cruelty, My Lord. Pray to Lord Jagannath, the Lord of the Universe; you can soon have peace.
KALAPAHAD	:	Impossible! Where there is no faithful Golap, there can be no peace. One, who has lost pious dutiful Tilottama, can have no peace.
TILOTTAMA	:	As long as there is your loyal wife goddess-

like Dulia is there, everything is possible. O Lord of my Life! Alas! Sister Dulia. I could not see you at this dying moment. (*Wounded Dulia enters.*)

DULIA : Where is the Lord of my Life? Oh, you are here. It's my good fortune that I could see my husband.

KALAPAHAD: Dulia, how is it that you are here? Why are you in such dress, Dulia? Why do you look so miserable?

DULIA : This is my good fate, Lord. It's my good fate that my husband is so worried. Uh, I am unable to sit - Golap! (*lying down*)

KALAPAHAD: My dear Dulia! My dear Tilottama!

DULIA : Tilottama! Where?

TILOTTAMA : Here, sister.

DULIA : Where? This is Golap. Is Golap –?

TILOTTAMA : Can't you recognise me, sister. I am Tilottama.

DULIA : Tilottama! Sister! (*embracing each other*)

TILOTTAMA : Come, sister, we have finished our duty. Let us take rest with the Lord of Peace. Ah, Lord of my Life! Give farewell to your maid servants. Oh, Lord Jagannath! May You show the good path to my husband! (*dies*)

DULIA : May my husband be blessed! Farwell, O Lord of my Life. (*dies*)

KALAPAHAD: Ha! Ha! Ha! (*laughing*), All are in rest. – Kalapahad is also in peace. Who are you? Are you not frightened? Aren't you afraid of Kalapahad? Look. – Look here. This hand has been stained with Hindu blood,

– Hindu flesh. This hand is stained with Tilottama's blood, – Dulia's blood. Aren't you afraid? How horrible is this figure? (*as if in hallucination*) It is running towards me with open mouth to swallow me. Wait, wait a little. (*closing his eyes*) What horrible laughter! What pathetic lamentation! Be quiet! Be quiet! (*closing his ears*) – Oh what pain! – Be at peace! – Be at peace! – No. – No. It's impossible! It's very difficult to stay here, in this holy place.
(*While about to leave, Shikhi and Manai with the cut-off-head of Mukunda Deb enter.*)

SHIKHI & MANAI : (*showing the cut-off-head of Mukunda Deb*) Everything is possible in this world, Nawab Saheb.
(*Kalapahad moves away to a distance in fear.*)

SHIKHI & MANAI : Don't fear, Nawab Saheb, the head is lifeless.

KALAPAHAD: Lifeless head! Lifeless! It looks as if alive. What a devilish stare! How terrible is the open mouth! (*closing his eyes*) Take it away from me.

SHIKHI : How shall I take it away, without rewards?

MANAI : Never, never without rewards.

KALAPAHAD: Take them away, soldiers. Give these traitors to the King, to State, to the Race their rewards.

SHIKHI & MANAI : Nawab Saheb!

KALAPAHAD: Take them away.
(*Soldiers take Shikhi & Manai away.*)
Ha! Ha! Ha! Ha! (*laughing*) What rewards! Stop Mukunda. Don't look at me like that.

I am not against the Hindus. – I'm not greedy of Hindu Blood. Dulia, don't shout at me, talk softly. – I am not a wife killer. – I am not a devil. Tilottama, be calm. – Don't scold me. – I am not a deserter of my wife. I am not an outcast. – *(pause)* What? What do I hear? I am the deserter of wife – I am the wife killer – I am the castaway. What is it? What do I see? This is a tub of fire – a cauldron full of boiling oil. Is it for my punishment? Impossible! Am I criminal to be punished? Am I sinner to be punished? I am innocent; I need to be redeemed. – I am pious; I need to be rewarded.

(*A soldier enters with the cut-off heads of Shikhi and Manai.*)

SOLDIER : Take your reward. (*Throws the heads and flees*)

KALAPAHAD: This is my reward. Nobody has any claim over it. It's not anybody's due. Are you jealous? Can you be as suitable a winner as me? Can you be as dutiful as me? Ha! Ha! Ha! (*laughing*) You cannot. You have no such ability. Then, why are you greedy; why are you jealous? You can only see — the stacks of rewards I have won. Tilottama's dead body is my reward — Dulia's dead body is my reward — Shikhi and Manai's heads are my rewards — Mukunda Dev's head is my reward — destruction of Hindus is my reward — Hindu's loss of freedom is my reward! (*Curtain*)

Black Eagle Books

www.blackeaglebooks.org
info@blackeaglebooks.org

Black Eagle Books, an independent publisher, was founded as a nonprofit organization in April, 2019. It is our mission to connect and engage the Indian diaspora and the world at large with the best of works of world literature published on a collaborative platform, with special emphasis on foregrounding Contemporary Classics and New Writing.

www.ingramcontent.com/pod-product-compliance
Lightning Source LLC
Chambersburg PA
CBHW060611080526
44585CB00013B/782